Zoom

Zoom

How 12 Exceptional Companies Are Navigating the Road to the Next Economy

James M. Citrin
Coauthor of *Lessons from the Top*

in collaboration with

Paul B. Brown and
Jason Baumgarten

with Illustrations by R. J. Matson

CURRENCY

DOUBLEDAY

NEW YORK LONDON TORONTO SYDNEY AUCKLAND

A CURRENCY BOOK

PUBLISHED BY DOUBLEDAY

a division of Random House, Inc.

1540 Broadway, New York, New York 10036

CURRENCY and DOUBLEDAY are

trademarks of Doubleday, a division of Random House, Inc.

Book design by Chris Welch

Library of Congress Cataloging-in-Publication Data

Citrin, James M.

Zoom : how 12 exceptional companies are navigating the road to the

next economy / James M. Citrin.—1st ed.

p. cm.

Includes bibliographical references and index.

1. Industrial management—United States—Case studies.

2. Information technology—United States—Management—Case studies.

3. Success in business—United States—Case studies. I. Title.

HD70.U5 C537 2001

658—dc21

2001042304

ISBN 0-385-50131-5

First Edition: February 2002

SPECIAL SALES

Currency books are available at special discounts for bulk purchases for
sales promotions or premiums. Special editions, including personalized
covers, excerpts of existing books, and corporate imprints, can be
created in large quantities for special needs. For more information,
write to Special Markets, Currency Books, 280 Park Avenue, 11th floor,
New York, New York 10017, or e-mail *specialmarkets@randomhouse.com*.

2 4 6 8 10 9 7 5 3 1

To my parents, Glenna and Harold Citrin,
who have provided a lifetime of love and support

Contents

Part III: HITTING THE OPEN ROAD
Weaving the 6 Success Factors together to navigate the road to the Next Economy   179

Zoom

Prologue

Writing *Zoom* over the period from early 1999 to late 2001 has been in many ways like trying to lead a company through these tumultous times. What began as an effort to distill leadership lessons from the "new" economy gave way to trying to divine winning company strategies after one of the most spectacular boom *and* bust cycles in economic history. And, just when I thought I had it all figured out and locked into the pages of this book, terror struck—then a war.

Suddenly the economy choked, and companies that had been swimming against the tide of a slowing marketplace were thrust into a struggle for mere survival. Every firm that emerges on the other side of recovery as a leader will be battle-scarred, and while most of the companies featured in this book should thrive, there is no guarantee that they all will. The case studies, descriptions of winning management principles and illustrations in *Zoom* make up snapshots of cultures, decisions, leaders, and styles taken at unique moments in time. While each case study identifies patterns of successful application of an enduring principle, no company or leader is immune from the perils of difficult current conditions.

Events in the right—or shall I say wrong—combination can overwhelm just about any business. But that does not change what the companies profiled in *Zoom* are attempting to do to survive and flourish as they charge their way to the Next Economy. The principles they individually espouse, taken together and implemented in concert, will continue to set tremendous results in motion.

As I reassess *Zoom*, the resonating message is that ***the formula for management success going forward is to combine the best of the old with the best of the new***. That is, enduring leadership principles, coupled with innovative execution principles enabled by technology and the Internet, will be the winning recipe for businesses across all industries. I hope you will find that *Zoom* makes this case in compelling, memorable, and entertaining ways.

Exceptional Companies Under Pressure

With that said, while all of the twelve companies profiled in *Zoom* are confronting challenges difficult to imagine in 1999 or 2000, here is a précis of the issues that face four of them specifically:

- Akamai Technologies and Commerce One: Facing increased pressure to transition to new business models focused on high-end solution sales to enterprise customers, both of these companies have had to make cost cutting a priority to reach profitability and balance capacity with decreased demand. While their challenges are different, Akamai and Commerce One continue to live by the principle "Go for Speed."

- The Motely Fool: Realigning its size and growth plans with the new market realities, The Motley Fool's CEO stepped down after raising capital, ensuring an orderly succession, shrinking the workforce, and reducing costs. As the Internet content and community company was caught in the "Perfect Storm" of shrunken advertising demand and dried-up capital markets, the company and its founders must now live by the learning principle and make it through the ultimate learning experience.

- Yahoo!: CEO Terry Semel and his team are under intense pressure to turn the venerable Internet portal around by diversifying revenue streams in light of the advertising collapse. While Wall Street is impatiently awaiting a bold new plan and progress against it, Yahoo! continues to experiment with new models, encouraging a different kind of risk taking.

Finding New Meaning in Our Work

Like all of us in the days following September 11, I found myself simultaneously mourning and trying to make sense of the horrific events that befell New York City, Washington, D.C., and America. I also found myself reflecting deeply on the implications of the terrorists attacks for this book. It is still relevant? Indeed, are management and leadership lessons of *any* sort still important now that our collective attention has turned to war and attacking the global scourge of terrorism?

I think the answer is yes.

I believe that *Zoom* can in fact be a small but concrete step in our effort to rebuild. As Mayor Rudolph Giuliani said, the best thing concerned citizens can do to help New York City in this time of need is to "Come visit us, have dinner at one of our restaurants, and take in a Broadway show." So, too, is it the case at the national level. Those of us in the business world need to once again make our companies perform at their peak levels. Doing so will help the economy and support the way of life that Americans and other free nations have come to appreciate with renewed vitality.

At a personal level, we also have the opportunity to reassess our careers and consider how the events change our views about what we do. Given that the terrorists were trying to extinguish our capitalist system altogether, we can take solace and renewed pride in pursuing business activities. As a manager, you have the opportunity to help align people's desire for a deeper sense of meaning to what they do every day. Now more than ever, doing so will tap into that reservoir of yearning that people have to make a positive impact on the world.

A Memorial

One of the business leaders who played a key part in the book lost his life on September 11. Thirty-one-year-old Daniel Lewin was the cofounder of Akamai Technologies, a company profiled in Chapter 3. He was on Flight 11 from Boston to Los Angeles when it struck the World Trade Center. Danny's indomitable spirit and technological brilliance underpin his high-tech company. All of those who knew him agree that whether concerning his company, business in general, or perhaps even this book, he would want everyone involved to move on with their lives at full speed so as to defy those who would do us harm. I hope that this book serves as a small tribute to Danny's memory and to everyone affected by the terrible events of September 11, 2001.

Jim Citrin
New Canaan, Connecticut
October 27, 2001

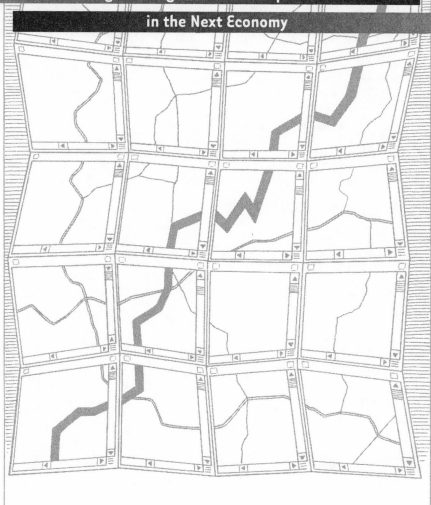

PART I

Unfolding the Map

Setting the stage for leadership and success

in the Next Economy

"Are we there yet?"

The trouble with our times is that the future is not
what it used to be.—*Paul Valéry*

"Are we there yet?" is a familiar and sometimes grating refrain for parents who take to the highways with their children. It's also the sentiment of many weary business travelers along the road to the era when technology, services, and knowledge combine to create a frictionless economy with seamless markets and price transparency. In such a Utopian world, information is readily available and infinitely searchable, and every product is custom-designed and produced as needed. The upshot: low inventory costs, improved quality, and lower prices. An ideal business scenario.

Are we *there* yet?

Trouble is, no one really knows where *there* is. Parents have an advantage: They know precisely where they're heading (most of the time). They know how long it will take, how much gas they'll need, and where they can stop to stretch their legs. Managers nowadays aren't so lucky.

For those of us struggling to apply the latest technologies, define new businesses, attract talented employees, and achieve profitable growth amid a difficult economy, unrelenting competition, and unforgiving capital markets, there is no simple road map to success. This is precisely why it's tougher than ever to be an effective leader and manager today. No one is going to fake their way through to sustainable success in the years ahead. And unfortunately, no one can prescribe easy remedies. They simply don't exist. The prickly problems are far too complex, and winning strategies are only beginning to emerge.

But it is possible to examine how some of the country's most visible companies are endeavoring to build thriving enterprises based on the new realities unleashed by technological changes, including the Internet. My research team and I have spoken with thousands of executives and pored over scores of companies. In the end we selected 12 to profile, including eBay, Sun Microsystems, Wal-Mart, Enron, Cisco Systems, and General Electric, to cull out specific and practical management lessons for today's business executives. It is my intent to strip away the jargon and management fads in the popular press to offer enduring ideas and strategies for tomorrow's emerging economy. These strategies are based on both timeless leadership principles and today's successful new management practices. Together, the blend of the lasting and the new make up the rules for navigating the road to the future. While they won't necessarily transform your business overnight, in time, these methods will help to build a more effective and confident management team in an era marked by unprecedented upheaval and uncertainty.

"Upheaval and uncertainty." This hasn't always been the best way to characterize American business. For most of the 20th century, businesses operated on calculated risk, and successful companies followed fairly predictable linear paths: Identify a niche, and then develop, market, and sell a product or service. The most significant challenges to the corporation used to be efficient manufacturing, cost containment, and consumer or industrial marketing. The major corporations that dominated the economy were asset-intensive operations that produced hard goods like automobiles or washing machines, resource-based products like oil, or infrastructure-laden services such as railroads or telephones. They transformed manufacturing into a science, gaining greater efficiencies every year. There were points along the business highway when other countries, such as Japan in the 1980s, surpassed American manufacturing abilities. But major U.S. companies eventually faced down that challenge and reasserted themselves.

This is not to belittle the business achievements of the last century. Efficient production, cost control, and effective marketing are tremendously complex challenges; but they are problems managers know and understand. They've lived with them for decades and leaders like Jack Welch of General Electric have built their legacies on them. Outsourcing. Vertical integration. Downsizing. Automation. All of these approaches have been deftly used in the war on cost. Market research, focus groups, brand extension, promotion, and advertising have been arrows in the marketing quiver for decades. Savvy managers are only getting better and better at cutting the fat from their operations and building on their established brands. In other words, when it comes to the major business challenges of the last century, we know the way.

But somewhere between the invention of the microchip and the first use of the words "hot link" everything changed. Cost faded as a primary focus of business and long-standing brand-building approaches lost their clout. What concerned American business in the nineties was not one particular scourge, but a bevy of difficult business conundrums: Technology that suddenly made it easier to hear from customers, but harder to assimilate their feedback; the fact that while capital flowed freely, it flowed to many players chasing the same idea, making it more difficult to earn a return on substantial investments; the proliferation of new competitors, striking mortal fear into all managers, only to disappear, in most cases, just as precipitously.

At the root of this rapidly changing landscape is digital technology. Some experts claim that technology is just another business tool, like a slide rule or a protractor. But it's a tool that comes with entirely new and onerous demands upon businesses and the people who use it. If they get it right, managers can help their organizations deal with the upheaval and uncertainty that typify today's environment. A business culture that grows up centered on digital technology is radically different from one that does not. Software applications, for example, are never completely finished; they are kicked out in versions. Customers respond to each version and the product is constantly updated and tweaked, with no finish line. Internet applications for business are the same way. Web sites, networking tools, and viral marketing programs are in a constant state of refinement and experimentation. Serendipitously, managers increasingly find success by trying a series of ideas and seeing which work best. And rapid prototyping and computer-aided design have brought similar management approaches to the manufacturing sector. Ford Motor Company, for example, doesn't need to build a car to test its fuel efficiency. Computer models take care of that. Pharmaceutical firms, likewise, can use 3-D molecular modeling to create new compounds that might turn into real drugs.

What we see evolving around these new technologies is nothing less than an entirely new corporate ethos: one that encompasses constant change, experimentation, failure, retooling, and finally, success—only to be reinvented yet again in the near future. While this new digital world can be challenging and nerve-racking, especially for those who like solid answers and definite goals, what we discovered is that managers *can* learn to cope with the uncertainty that comes with experimentation, and define the boundaries of a business that must fluidly and frequently morph into something else.

Even success itself has become more conditional in today's world. On the one hand, many of the companies profiled in *Zoom* encourage their employees to fail. Yet executives are under increasing pressure to show results for their actions. If you succeed one quarter, the goals are set higher for the next. And if your company fails to meet its goals, its stock will be pummeled. The bar is constantly set higher on every front—including your customers. Fabled Silicon Valley marketer Regis McKenna points out that the more you give a consumer, the more he or she expects from you. If you deliver a package overnight, customers soon expect same-day delivery. Executive management has discovered that the corporate board is not much different. Give them results and they want better results, faster.

Rising expectations can also lead to rapidly deflated stock prices on Wall Street when these expectations aren't met. As we've seen in the last year, billions of dollars of net worth can be obliterated in a matter of days. When AT&T announced in May 2000 that its growth rate would be 1% less than the consensus estimate on Wall Street, it lost 15% of its market value—$27 billion, in a single day— paving the way for the break-up of the venerable corporation. Dramatic though that was, it was still less than half as large as the 35% collapse in market value that Procter & Gamble suffered several months earlier for similarly missing growth estimates, an event that contributed to former Chief Executive Officer Durk Jager losing his job. When Apple Computer warned that disappointing sales of new products would cause its profit in the fiscal fourth quarter of 2000 to fall short of forecasts, the company's stock fell an astounding 52%, cleaving over $9 billion off its $17 billion market value. And Cisco Systems, universally acclaimed for its growth and innovation, reached the pinnacle of corporate success on March 27, 2000, when its $550 billion market capitalization gave it the honor as the most valuable public company; by April 6, 2001, barely a year later, it had crashed 83%. Its precipitous decline was driven by a slowdown in capital spending, which forced the company to write off $2.5 billion for excess inventory, lay off 8,500 workers, and deal with a 30% third-quarter 2001 revenue decline.

With each new round of earnings disappointments, there are a spate of CEO departures. According to the outplacement firm Challenger, Gray & Christmas, chief executives have been leaving their companies at an accelerating pace in recent years. For the second half of 1999, approximately 50 CEOs left their companies per month, on average. But in 2000, the rate rose to nearly 90 per month. In October 2000, more than 125 CEOs were forced out or retired from their companies, including such major corporations as Lucent Technologies, Gillette, and Maytag Corporation.

Expect more bloodshed in the years ahead. For while companies may hope for a quick payoff from their enormous technology investments of recent years, chances are that returns on investment will take longer than most expect. Speaking at a recent technology conference, Andy Grove, chairman of Intel, claimed that the industry trends we are seeing today are exactly analogous to trends that emerged in the 1970s, when Grove and other high-tech CEOs successfully convinced corporate America to invest in technology to compete with the Japanese and gain greater efficiency. But the payoff from the investment took far longer than corporations expected, and by the 1980s, many were unhappy with their high-tech expenditures. As a result, technology spending began to slow, sending companies like Intel into a quandary. Grove claims that the Internet is now having its "1980s." "People expect to generate a return from going online, but the return always takes longer than people wish, and then they get frustrated and disappointed," says Grove.

The truth is, many companies feel they have already been waiting an awfully long time for the power of information technology and networked computing to streamline our businesses. The first significant shift began in the early 1980s, as *Business Week* and *Fortune* magazines reported, when we entered an era where services and knowledge for the first time outpaced tangible outputs. Since then, employment in the manufacturing sector has fallen from nearly 40% of total employment in 1950 to less than 18% in 2000, while service sector employment has grown from less than 14% in 1950 to more than 35% today, with the inflection point occurring in the mid-1980s.

By 1995 the trends driving the information age were feeding off themselves and the Internet supercharged the economy and captured the attention of a global audience already thinking about how information and knowledge had become the cornerstones of their professional and personal lives. The date that many on Wall Street and in Silicon Valley realized something significant was under way was August 9, 1995, when a tiny software company with no visible profits named Netscape was taken public. In an incredible IPO, driven by enormous buzz, Netscape's stock skyrocketed on its first trading day and gave notice to the investing public of the promise of this new thing called the Internet. The ensuing boom and later bust of the dot.com–driven new economy shattered managers' understanding of the formulas for success and left a hole in their confidence as gaping as that in the portfolios managed by the formerly hot money managers.

A TALE OF TWO ECONOMIES

For nearly a decade it was hard to imagine things getting much better economically. The United States enjoyed the longest continuous economic expansion in its history. Until recently, U.S. unemployment rates have been at a historic low and income at almost all levels has risen over the past decade. The median household income in the United States is now over $40,000 a year, the highest in our nation's history (in constant dollars). Labor shortages have been common, especially among knowledge workers, a sector in which the

U.S. unemployment rate hovers well below 2%. And the market for talented professionals, while much softer than in 1999 and 2000, still retains attractive fundamentals.

Yet on the other hand, the economy was sent reeling in 2000 and 2001. After an 18-year bull market run, when the Dow Jones Industrial Average rose from 777 on August 12, 1982, to an all-time high of 11,723 on January 14, 2000 (a 16% annualized increase), the index fell nearly 10% by April 30, 2001. And after the technology-heavy Nasdaq Index, which rose from 483 to 5,048 in the 8 years ending March 31, 2000 (a 34% annualized increase), crashed 67% from its high point by April 4, 2001. The fall of the Nasdaq Index is all the more sobering when you consider that the Great Crash of October 1929 sent the Dow down 44% and that Black Monday, October 19, 1987, drove the Dow down a relatively modest 22.6%.

Beyond the financial markets there is disturbing news as well. There were 1.4 million bankruptcies in the year ended June 30, 2001—an increase of over 400% since 1980—which broke all records. Our personal saving rate, which was as high as 10.6% as a percentage of disposable personal income in 1984, is now in the negative column, and at a 53-year low. The income disparity between the wealthiest and poorest citizens is at an all-time high, which, many argue, portends serious social and societal challenges.

Through the dot.com era, with regard to business and the economy, we swung from great optimism to great despair. At one point, in March 2000, a nationwide poll conducted by accounting and consulting firm Ernst and Young reported that 74% of 2000's college seniors believed they would become millionaires in their lifetimes. Yet a mere month later, *New York* magazine perfectly captured the economic downturn with a cover headline that read: "Dot's All Folks!"

It is no wonder that it seems as if we have been traveling to the future of the new economy for a long time now. Many executives are becoming impatient—losing faith in the technology they've paid so dearly to acquire and becoming a bit flustered by the relentless change that they've been forced to absorb. The continual introduction of newer, more powerful, computer and communications hardware and software has increased the need for employees and management to develop new skills and knowledge; increasingly, many companies seem to be frozen in place, waiting for the future to unfold, rather than proactively trying to take charge of an uncertain environment and future. Companies are unsure of how to proceed, whether to embrace the new technologies and the ideas and strategies forged in the cauldron of the Internet, or whether to fall back safely on traditional approaches and thinking. It is what Alvin Toffler best described, nearly a quarter of a century ago, as *Future Shock:* "The dizzying disorientation brought on by the premature arrival of the future." Gregory Papadopoulos, chief technology officer of Sun Microsystems, echoed the dizzying rate of change, when he told me that "thirty percent of the knowledge generated inside our company is obsolete within a year."

Even in a world of uncertainty, however, we can be sure of certain things: death, taxes, and Moore's Law—that the power of the microchip would double every year (later the law was amended to every two years). With technology increasingly embedded in all aspects of business, the relentless march of Moore's Law and the introduction of new technologies compound the need for managers to help their organizations cope rather than just maintain the status quo.

The Internet sparked the emergence of companies like Amazon.com, Yahoo!, and eBay, which grew in a matter of years to be market dominators. And for a time, larger traditional brick-and-mortar companies seemed to act as if they were deer caught in headlights.

Eventually, however, large companies began to counterattack.

Some, like Maytag's ill-fated Brandwise venture or Disney's Go.com portal, made aggressive bets only to come up short. But others found the formula for success.

Charles Schwab, for example, which co-CEO David Pottruck defines as a "technology company that happens to be in the brokerage business," saw the Internet as a breakthrough that would irrevocably change the heart and soul of its business. In January 1998, spurred on by the momentum of E*Trade, then the leading online broker, Schwab brought its skunk-works e-Schwab project into its core business and offered online trading to all of its 1.2 million customers for the discount price of $29.95 per trade. The company simultaneously dramatically cut commission rates in its offline business in order to equal its rates for online transactions. This was a bet-the-company decision, but the gamble quickly paid off. In the next 5 months, Schwab attracted new customers at the fastest rate in its history, opening up more than half a million new accounts and capturing $40 billion in new customer assets. They also learned that their real world presence was an enormous asset, something the pure Internet brokers could never match. Part of Schwab's success, and the reason why it is such a powerful role model for other companies today, is that they learned how to juggle the difficult balance between driving certain activities to the Internet while encouraging other essential activities to remain in the offline world. Today, for example, while 86% of its transactions are executed online, 70% of new customer accounts are opened at one of Schwab's 363 *brick-and-mortar* retail branches. The company recognized that when individuals are entrusting their savings to a financial institution, it is a powerful human desire to want to kick the tires, look the company's professionals in the eye, and develop a feeling of security about where they are placing their assets. On the other hand, Schwab learned that once this decision is made, customers prefer to execute their trades, which are commodity transactions, online.

And like America Online's 2000 acquisition of Time Warner,

Schwab took advantage of its high market valuation and P/E ratio (51x) to acquire the esteemed U.S. Trust Company and capture its $133 billion of assets under management and add the 147-year-old company's top echelon clientele and renowned brand name to Schwab's business. Today, Schwab's market capitalization is $25 billion, or 10 times that of E*Trade's $2.5 billion—a dramatic widening of the gap from April 1999, when Schwab's value was less than 4 times more valuable. The company's customer centric strategy, fully integrated online and offline distribution, and breadth of clientele—from low-end to top-end—has put them in the major leagues of the investment industry. Schwab's hybrid bricks-and-clicks strategy gives it an enormous cash flow and profit advantage relative to pure Internet brokerage houses, which cannot match its range of products, services, and valuable physical presence. Its Internet strategy also put enormous pressure on traditional Wall Street powerhouses such as Goldman Sachs, Merrill Lynch, and Morgan Stanley, which, because of their commission structures and internal resistance to cannibalizing their brokers' businesses, were slower to move to the Internet. In fact, Merrill Lynch, the nation's largest brokerage firm, was driven by Schwab to do a 180-degree about-face regarding its Internet strategy. In December 1998, when Schwab's market capitalization narrowly surpassed that of Merrill ($25.5 billion versus $25.4 billion), it provided the burning platform for Merrill Lynch to shift its public position—from the Internet being a "danger to the health of the U.S. financial system," to the announcement of an integrated suite of online and offline products and services. To Merrill's credit, the venerable firm drew on the enormous power of its brand, financial resources, and history of exceptional client service to effectively implement its own bricks-and-clicks strategy. As a result, Merrill Lynch has recaptured its historic market-value advantage over Schwab (by $14 billion as of May 2001).

Schwab's transformation roughly mirrors the greater shift in power over the last two years from IPO start-ups back to traditional, profitable companies. Until the Nasdaq began to tank, big companies had been struggling to deal with the impact of the Internet on their business models and organizations. Today, traditional companies have been regaining the high ground. Still the ground they have reclaimed has irrevocably shifted. Rather than resisting the impact of the Internet and the strategies that have evolved based on speed, convenience, and efficiency, the most successful companies in today's transformational economy have embraced it and made it their own. As Jack Welch and GE's chief information officer and e-commerce czar Gary Reiner put it, "Dot.coms, the small companies that everyone thought could maintain the first mover's advantage, began with no revenues, but plenty of costs—for advertising, warehousing, staffing up and more. They were therefore totally revenue dependent and, as the huge number that were forced to file for Chapter 11 reminds us, their breakeven was always uncertain at best."

Of course, this sounds like wisdom graced by the benefit of hindsight. But Welch has been saying this since late 1999, before the Internet companies began their free fall. The best companies have realized that just because market forces have brought the dot.com era crashing to an end, it doesn't mean that the new ideas and approaches to doing business they helped to pioneer should be cast aside too. Instead, the most forward-looking companies, as we'll see in the cases of the companies profiled in this book, have absorbed the best of their principles and strategies and applied them to their traditional business practices.

Increasingly, for the companies profiled in this book, the Internet has become a vital piece of their technology and business strategy. The best companies tightly lash it to virtually every aspect of how they do business. But it takes a lot of planning, trial and error, and execution to pull it off successfully.

And that is precisely what *Zoom* zeroes in on.

One of the great challenges of writing a book like this is putting all of the firsthand experience we've learned from working with

> Even in a time of unrelenting, technology-driven change and uncertainty, there *is* a formula for management success. Today's most successful management teams combine the enduring principles of leadership that Tom Neff and I first distilled in *Lessons from the Top*, based on one-on-one interviews with the 50 most successful business leaders in America, with the hard-won new rules of successful execution that today's market-leading companies have learned and adopted from the rise of technology and the Internet. Together, these enduring principles of leadership and execution have forged a new path for managers attempting to successfully navigate their way from today's changing business environment to the business world of tomorrow. It is this new amalgam of old and new that *Zoom* attempts to explore, as we race ever faster into the future.

many of the world's leading companies and managers into a framework that will help other companies and managers better navigate their way to the future. I happened upon an unusual model for inspiration—Robert M. Pirsig's *Zen and the Art of Motorcycle Maintenance*. At first blush, that book is about a journey. Pirsig looked at one set of things—a motorcycle, the countryside, and a road trip with his son and a couple of friends—and yet, in doing so, saw deeply below the surface to something more enduring.

In *Zoom*, too, my goal is to see beyond the distracting noise of running a business to unearth and address the hard, long-term business questions that every company and manager face—from speeding up decision-making and execution without sacrificing performance to keeping employees focused on doing the right things even as the company goes about changing the way it does business. Lest the Pirsig book seem too unlikely a model, in the next chapter, I'll even show you how the motorcycle plays into all of this as well.

CHAPTER 2

The Six Factors for Success in the Next Economy

Combining Enduring Leadership Principles with E-Commerce Management Strategies

I f Wolfgang Amadeus Mozart and Elton John traded places in history, would Mozart have become the biggest rock star of our day? Would Elton John have been the greatest composer of all time? Both men were blessed with perfect musical pitch, a prodigious work ethic, spectacular manual dexterity, and driving ambition. One composed *Eine Kleine Nachtmusik (A Little Night Music)* and charmed the royal courts of Europe in the late 1700s, while the other, composing the popular music of his era, wrote "Candle in the Wind," played to sellout crowds in Madison Square Garden, and gave expression to the world's grief at Princess Diana's funeral.

Would Mozart and Elton John have been equally successful if their lives and times had been transposed? Certainly their talents and genius are quite different, and I would never burden any modern artist with the mantle of genius that rests so securely on the shoulders of Mozart. Nonetheless, the very qualities of creative rebellion, musical insight, sheer determination, and raw talent that each share would, I suggest, make each successful in whatever age they lived in.

I would argue that the same is true of world-class business leaders as well. Let's consider, for example, Jack Welch and Scott McNealy. Welch joined General Electric as a staffer in 1960, fresh from earning his Ph.D. from the University of Illinois. At that time, the company was one of the largest manufacturers in the world. However, over the years, it became bloated and slow to react to competition from abroad. During Welch's tenure as CEO from 1981 to 2001, the company slashed costs dramatically, pried open new markets, became an operationally exceptional company, made significant acquisitions, and drove its market value from $12 billion to $500 billion, making it the most valuable public company on the planet and securing Welch's place as the era's most famous and respected leader.

On the other side of the country, CEO Scott McNealy, a generation behind Jack Welch, has taken Sun Microsystems from an unknown start-up in 1984 to a computer industry behemoth today. The company's high-end computer servers and software form the backbone of the Internet, and the company's market capitalization soared from $64 million at its March 1986 IPO to $1.8 billion in 1990 to $57 billion as of May 2001.

Would McNealy and Welch, two of today's business legends (and golfing buddies), have been as successful if they traded places or had faced each other's challenges?

Once again, I would argue, yes.

Like great musicians, great business leaders, from Henry Ford to Michael Dell, share a surprising number of characteristics. In my previous book, *Lessons from the Top*, coauthored with Spencer Stuart's U.S. Chairman, Tom Neff, we systematically identified, interviewed, and profiled the CEOs our research suggested were the 50 most successful business leaders in America. Our analysis was based on a Gallup survey of 575 business leaders, detailed financial analysis of 10 years of data for the largest 1,000 U.S. public companies measuring cash flow relative to capital employed, and total returns to shareholders. We then ranked the leaders against these qualitative and quantitative data and prioritized a very long list into the 50 best. The methodology we developed, executed in 1997 and 1998, has proven its accuracy by withstanding the test of time. While any such list represents a particular point in time, as of the writing of this book, *not one* of the 50 business leaders in the book have been ousted from their positions, which is remarkable in today's environment of ever-shorter CEO tenures. The key discovery we made as a result of our intensive, one-on-one discussions with these top 50 CEOs was that each of these outstanding leaders follow a number of common principles. In fact, there are 6 principles in all, which distilled to their essence are to:

1. *Live with integrity and lead by example.* Integrity is the internal sense of right and wrong that should direct everything that a successful person does. Living with integrity and leading by example build the trust in senior management that is common among— and critical for—high-performing organizations.

2. *Develop a winning strategy or big idea.* In an age of increasing competitive intensity, a leader must be the source of creating a winning strategy, based on a company's competitive advantages and fundamental customer needs. Not only must leaders come up with a big idea, it must be the right idea. There are many companies that came up with a big idea that was wrong or for which the timing was off. The key is to go to the company's roots and build on the things the organization truly does best and link this to

what matters most to customers (defined by what they will pay for).

3. *Build a great management team.* As Michael Dell told me, "One person cannot do anything alone." The best business leaders have all, to one extent or another, built highly successful management teams around complementary skills and shared values. In no case is the priority of creating a great management team more important than with entrepreneurs attempting to break their companies through from start-ups to successful, sustainable, large corporations.

4. *Inspire employees to achieve greatness.* Employees today are looking for deeper meaning from their work. As a result, the most successful business leaders know how to tap into employees' deepest motivations and desires, by showing them the higher purpose of their organization's mission and by empowering them, being supportive, and getting out of their way.

5. *Organize for flexibility and responsiveness.* In our interview with Jack Welch, he called it, "The power of informal." With today's information technology facilitating instantaneous global communications, the successful business leaders will be those who break down slow, overly formalized hierarchies and decision-making processes. The key is to have the right people solving problems no matter where they are located geographically or hierarchically in the organization.

6. *Implement reinforcing management systems.* Tying all of the principles together are the performance measurements, compensation practices, and information systems that a company uses to operate itself. To be most effective, these management systems need to be consistent with and reinforce the values and strategy of the organization.

Taken together, we described these principles as *Doing the Right Things Right.* Our research showed that these traits were the cornerstones of success—at both the individual and organizational levels. And they are as true today as they were 50 years ago. Because the principles are inexorably linked, with each helping to buttress and reinforce the next, we expressed these concepts as a circle, or "Business Leadership Wheel."

However, during the last three years, in the heyday of easy venture capital funding, investment madness, and cult-worship of Internet entrepreneurs, it seemed as if these basic principles had become quaintly old-fashioned, and indeed had fallen out of favor. An entire generation of go-go young managers and executives seemed to spring up from nowhere with new rules and new methods for building companies and wealth. These so-called pioneers cast aside traditional management tenets to embrace an entirely different way of doing business. They rejected corporate hierarchies, ascribed to a 24/7 business philosophy, spent capital as if it were in endless supply, and focused more on generating traffic and capturing market share than earning a profit. And, oddly enough, for a brief moment, it seemed as if they'd gotten it right.

Today, of course, with dot.coms piled up like car wrecks on the new-economy trash heap, those brash young entrepreneurs don't seem as all-knowing or wise. It is tempting to think that the whole

new-economy craze was a terrific mistake, and that the new strategies that the dot.com generals evolved will recede into oblivion like
the 8-track tape. Pundits are now comparing the speculative frenzy
of the Internet boom to the famous tulip craze which captivated
Dutch society at the end of the 18th century and left a raft of otherwise sensible Dutch business people broke. As author Gary Hamel
recently said, "Aside from Internet cultists and shameless IT vendors, there's scarcely anyone left on the planet who would utter the
words 'new economy' without a snort of cynical derision."

*Was the dot.com insurgency just a youthful paroxysm that could never
successfully substitute for good old traditional management know-how?*

The answer isn't so black and white. Before executives take solace
in the expectation that things can finally get "back to normal," they
need to realize what a dangerous trap this would be. Technology has
become such a deeply imbedded and intricate part of our lives that
we take for granted all of its manifestations—from e-mail to cell
phones to voice-mail to laptops to the Internet. The truth is, the digital economy will remain a driving force in business for years to
come. Moreover, some of the new rules that these young turks—and
the Internet companies they were building—wrote have dramatically changed how people work and managers manage.

When you strip away both the precrash hype and postcrash doom
surrounding the Internet, is there anything left?

Something called the *"Next* Economy."

What exactly do I mean by the Next Economy?[1] I contend that it
represents the coming together of enduring principles and new
strategies—bricks and clicks. Some of the governing principles
guiding the companies leading the way into the future, such as those
that we described as *Doing the Right Things Right,* are as old as business itself. But they turn out to be only half the story. There are new

1. The term Next Economy was coined in a February 2001 article in *Fast
Company* magazine.

factors for success that address and embrace the fundamental changes unleashed by new technology and the Internet. The Next Economy can be described by three emerging realizations:

First, companies are increasingly appreciating that the Internet needs to be woven into every aspect of its operations. While the Internet is no longer considered "a business" in and of itself, managers must recognize the Internet for what it is—and is not—and use it accordingly. E-mail, for example, is one obvious Internet communications tool that has changed the way colleagues and customers interact. When coupled with the Internet, database marketing and customer relationship management allow companies to address customers individually, and yet on a mass basis. The Internet is also an information management collection and management system, allowing vast stores of knowledge to be accessed and used at a moment's notice. It is a channel of distribution as well, where products and services can be offered for sale along with other forms of commerce. Winning companies, for example, are driving a growing proportion of their commercial orders to secure Web sites, which allow them to get the paperwork right the first time, take costs down, and improve customer service. Companies are finding that the greatest power of technology and the Internet, however, is not to automate preexisting functions or processes. Instead, its power is to give businesses the ability to do things that previously could not be done.

Second, companies now realize that they should treat the Internet adage, "get big fast," with an enormous grain of salt. Managers need to concentrate on driving revenue, profit, and risk-adjusted return on capital invested. They need to make sure that the company has viable options for financing long-term growth. Overall, the future of the Internet lies in economically viable new businesses that both satisfy a demand and allow fundamentally new forms of commerce, collaboration, and learning.

Third, in the Next Economy neither upstarts nor traditional companies can count on attracting all the talent. The headlong rush of professionals and MBAs into new ventures built on dreams and promises of IPO riches is over. But they are not necessarily rushing back into the same old companies. The most desirable employees will seek employment with those companies that they perceive as having the best competitive prospects, corporate cultures, and opportunities for personal growth and professional development. A company can no longer sustain itself on the shoulders of a charismatic leader alone. As has been the case for decades, it is essential for companies to build an outstanding management team populated by people with complementary skills and shared values. And professionals who want to be great business leaders themselves need to gain the experience from being a part of a winning management team. In tight times, people still need to feel that they are part of something worthwhile and growing. If a company lays off 10% of its workforce, it will have to work harder to inspire those who remain. And this can be brutally challenging in a slumping or seesaw economy.

How does a company win amid the realities of the Next Economy?

The road to success among the companies I've profiled in this book has been achieved by applying the new factors for success that have evolved in today's digital age while remaining true to the enduring principles of management and leadership. In other words, managers will need to apply the best of the old and the best of the new, much like the modern-day university library, which intermingles archival, documentary source materials in physical form with the vast treasures of digitized material accessible online. Nowadays, one without the other is incomplete and suboptimal.

Of the companies that are leading the way combining e-business and traditional business strategies, we are beginning to see winning formulas emerge. And that is what I have tried to describe and distill in *Zoom*—identifying the winning strategies from today's exceptional companies, and showing how they come to life in the real world.

In researching this book, I took a multipronged approach. First, with the help of my research team and half a dozen Spencer Stuart colleagues, I conducted literally thousands of conversations with executives, board directors, and industry analysts, which helped solicit recommendations for outstanding companies successfully navigating their way on the road to the Next Economy. I also drew analytical support, in terms of examining corporate financial performance and shareholder returns, from the research team at Lazard Asset Management, a division of Lazard Frères. And of course, I also relied on my own professional experience as the managing director of Spencer Stuart's Global Technology, Communications, and Media Practice, which provides me with access to many of the world's most influential leaders and thinkers in business today.

My objective was to identify a *cross-section of winning companies* in today's economy, from early-stage success stories to *Fortune* 50 companies. It was not to choose the 12 "best" companies, nor the 12 most valuable, nor the 12 largest. Any such list would have been out of date as soon as the analysis was complete. Instead, I wanted to identify a diverse range of companies drawn from various industries, and at different stages of development, to study how different companies are pursuing innovative and successful approaches to today's business challenges. I was looking for some companies that are known for particular strengths, such as Cisco Systems' deal-making machine, or eBay's powerful online business model, or General Electric's famed capability to execute. I also wanted to study how some old economy stalwarts such as General Motors were applying the Internet to their operations, and transforming their business as a result of today's changing business environment. The result is a group of companies from a wide-ranging set of industries—finance, retail, automotive, media, diversified industrial, and high technology. Some, like GE, GM, Wal-Mart, Sun Microsystems, eBay, Cisco, and Yahoo!, are household names; others, such as BEA Systems, Akamai Technologies, The Motley Fool, Commerce One,

and StorageNetworks, are much less widely known, but also successful in their market segments and business practices.

With each company, I conducted in-depth one-on-one interviews
with the CEOs and other top executives in order to distill the best
practices that differentiate each Next Economy market leader
from the scores of companies that have stalled or failed to take advantage of the technology and ideas that have emerged in recent
years. As a result of these interviews and research, I discovered that
each company shares certain key characteristics that distinguish
them from their competitors. In the end, six common strategies
emerged from my research into these Next Economy leaders. These
six strategies, or factors for success, can be distilled to their essence
as follows:

1. Go for speed.
2. Create a learning organization.
3. Obsess the customer.
4. Reward—don't punish—appropriate risk-taking and failure.
5. Absorb uncertainty.
6. Master deal-making and partnering skills.

These new principles will be detailed in Part II of the book and
illustrated with company case studies. I'll show you, for example:

- Why the need for speed is driven by economic realities, and how
  companies like Akamai Technologies have learned to move at a
  lightning pace.
- Why it is critical to move beyond the lip service of training and
  development and create a true *learning* organization. A company
  like eBay is continuously learning from its fanatical community of
  users and evolving its business and operations in response to their
  needs.
- Why the power of the customer is greater than ever before and

how companies like Sun Microsystems put the customer at the epicenter of its organization.

- Why experimentation, risk-taking, and failure are essential to allowing a company to innovate and grow and how companies like Wal-Mart can become market leaders following this tenet.

- Why employees need a management team that can absorb the wrenching uncertainty of change around them. I'll look at how General Motors, for example, organizes itself in a way that simultaneously liberates employees and keeps them calm and focused, even in the midst of one of the most rattling market downturns in history.

- Why partnering and deal-making are essential core competencies in the Next Economy. Cisco Systems grew to become one of the world's most valuable companies by swiftly acquiring and integrating dozens of companies over the years.

- How a company like GE is able to pull all of the strategies together and execute them successfully against any number of smaller, supposedly swifter niche rivals.

Building a lasting and successful company often means weathering abrupt and brutal changes in the market, including economic downturns. Despite this, the companies that I have selected for *Zoom* have achieved outstanding returns for investors in recent years. When taken as a whole, the 12 companies that my team and I examined in this book offered investors a cumulative return of 466.5% over the five years from 1996 to 2000 (see chart on page 28). The S&P 500 composite index, by comparison, returned only 114% during the same period. Yes, the year of 2000 and the first three quarters of 2001 were not pretty for technology stocks, or most any stock for that matter, but their losses must be seen against the backdrop of widely based market declines, where, in 2000, the Dow Jones Industrials lost 6%, the S&P 500 lost 10%, and the Nasdaq lost 39%. The Nasdaq, in fact, crashed 67% from its March 30, 2000, high to

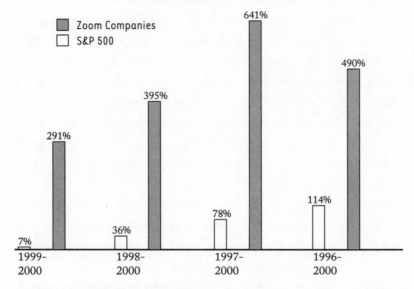

Zoom Companies Returns vs. the Market
(Total Cumulative Shareholder Returns)

Note: Includes all *Zoom* companies that were public during the noted time period: From 1996 onward, Cisco Systems, General Electric, Sun Microsystems, General Motors, and Wal-Mart Stores; from 1997 onward, Yahoo!; from 1998 onward, BEA Systems; from 1999 onward, eBay; from 2000 Akamai Technologies, StorageNetworks, and Commerce One. One company that is private and therefore excluded from this analysis is The Motley Fool.

Source: Lazard Asset Management and Spencer Stuart analysis.

its low on April 4, 2001, the largest such drop in its 30-year history. Nonetheless, many of the market leaders have already begun their climb back to superior growth and returns.

As you will see, each of these companies continues to adapt quickly to changes and assimilate knowledge at an astounding pace. The key success factors that give them a competitive advantage are strategies other companies can apply to their own organizations. I've drawn these success factors as a second, self-reinforcing circle—or what I refer to as a "Business Execution Wheel."

These new principles don't exist alone. They are effective only to the extent that they accompany the lasting principles of leadership that have guided so many companies' triumphs over the years. Both

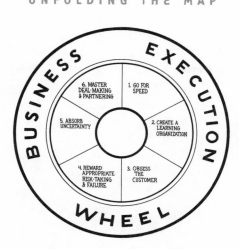

of the wheels of business success must be utilized for a company to maximize its potential in the years ahead. Like the two wheels of Pirsig's motorcycle that I referred to in chapter 1, these two wheels work in tandem. Each is vital to roll smoothly down the road to the future.

But how do the wheels work in practice? In the next section, you'll begin to find out.

PART II
Signposts Along the Way

The 6 factors for success illustrated by case studies of a cross-section of Next Economy winners

Introduction to Part II

Part II is the heart of this book. It is here that the wheels of business success meet the road. In this section, my goal is to vividly show how these principles—or success factors—take shape in the 12 winning companies that I've analyzed—and how these principles may be applied to your own organization.

Each chapter in Part II incorporates two company case studies to illustrate the specific success factor the chapter addresses, as well as offering 10 specific implementation points.

As you read through each case study, patterns should begin to emerge. You'll notice how each of the companies, in its own way, achieves speed, obsesses on the customer, creates the feedback loops to enable learning, and follows the other principles.

Successfully navigating the road to the Next Economy is about focusing on all of the aspects of execution—and doing so in a way that is effective, given your company's strategy and culture.

It will be useful to keep two key questions in mind as you read each case study:

1. Is the company likely to remain successful five years out?
2. Would *you* want to work there?

The companies we've studied depend on intellectual capital to drive them forward—knowledge assets are their most important resource. This fact may seem peripheral to a company's success, but it's not. If you take a look at the recent job market statistics, despite the recent softening, the challenges ahead quickly come into high relief. According to the U.S. Census Bureau, the year 2000 was when the final wave of baby boomers peaked—right now there are still a flood of managers in their mid-thirties to mid-forties. But by 2015 there will be 15% fewer members of this age group than today.

This means that the traditional pool from which top managers are drawn in the coming years will be smaller than at any time in 25 years. But if the economy grows at a rate of 3% to 4% per year, projections show that the number of management and leadership positions required will be approximately 67% higher in 2015 than today.

The interplay of these two trends—shorter supply and greater demand—will set off what consulting firm McKinsey & Company dubbed the War for Talent. And it's coming at a difficult time. According to Merrill Lynch, in 1980 the price-to-book value ratio of the 10 largest publicly traded companies was 1.2x. Today, it is more than 12.1x, or 10 times greater. The explanation for this change is simple. The financial markets have come to acknowledge the value of the intellectual capital that is housed within those corporations. And most of that capital is locked inside the heads of the people who work there. As Bill Gates has said, "Take our 20 best people away, and I can tell you that Microsoft would become a much less important company."

The bottom line is that talented executives will continue to be in short supply and strong demand. Corporations will be under intense pressure to retain top-performing employees and attract new ones. A winning human capital management strategy—one that successfully attracts, develops, retains, and rewards people—is rapidly becoming one of the most important competitive advantages an organization can have.

Building a winning company that can attract and retain the best people depends on setting a strong foundation while still being flexible enough to maneuver quickly and take on new challenges. That's what the motorcycle metaphor is all about—two sets of leadership and management principles that together can help transform your company from a collection of spare parts to a versatile, fast-paced machine.

The most talented individuals want to be part of a successful team and feel as if they are working toward important and common goals. This is what's required of every successful company in the Next Economy—whatever direction it ultimately takes.

CHAPTER 3

Success Factor #1
Go for Speed

Introduction

G et big fast. Achieve critical mass. Manage through ever-shortening product life cycles. Work 70 hours a work.

Speed has become a watchword of the Internet era. Bob Davis, the founder and former CEO of Lycos, who turned a $2 million investment into a $5.4 billion company reaching 91 million people in 41 countries, devoted an entire book, *Speed Is Life*, to the topic. Why all the emphasis on speed? Is there a *real* need to be quick and nimble, or have managers been deluded by the hype? Are they fighting paper dragons?

The old saw says that the race goes to the swift. Never before has that adage been more appropriate. Sure, many upstart companies dashed off to quick success only to discover that they couldn't sustain the effort. The fact is that speed will never mask poor management, faulty assumptions, or just plain sloppy execution. But for an organization to be a winner—and not an also-ran in the Next Economy—it must be fleet-footed.

In some instances speed and quick thinking have allowed relatively unknown companies to rise above their larger more established competitors. It was not that long ago that America-On-Line (as it was originally called after its 1985 founding) was not much more than a punch line—"training wheels for the Internet," as the cognoscenti called it. But seemingly overnight, CEO Steve Case, Bob Pittman, and the rest of their team built a massive brand that now rules the largest media company on the planet. Even before it acquired Time Warner, the company's market capitalization was 50% greater than that of the venerable Walt Disney Company.

Speed is, in fact, more important than ever as we enter the Next Economy, because the value between first- and second-place corporations is vastly different. The table on pages 39 and 40 shows that the top two players in the traditional economy are relatively close in value. Not so in the digital world. Here the market leader gets a huge premium. eBay's recent $10 billion market capitalization is a whopping 2,272% greater than its closest analogue, Priceline. On average, the top companies in the digital economy have over 3,000% larger market values than their second-place opponents. For traditional companies, the margin for the same comparison is just over 200%.

What happens when the market contracts?

Survival of the fittest; a flight to quality.

As the table demonstrates, the value gap between the top 2 players has stayed relatively flat for traditional leaders amid the wild gyrations between the third quarter of 2000 and the second quarter of 2001, while the gap has widened greatly among digital economy leaders.

Why is this the case?

Table 1 Market Value Gaps Between #1 and #2 for Selected Sectors*
Market Values – $ millions

	"Traditional Economy"				"Digital Economy" Value		
Company	09/26/00	12/31/00	02/28/01	Company	09/26/00	12/31/00	02/28/01
Airlines				**Online Services**			
Southwest Airlines	$11,800	$16,905	$14,066	America Online	$128,700	$81,175	$102,705
Delta Airlines	$5,600	$6,171	$5,179	@Home	$5,700	$2,236	$2,349
Value Gap	**211%**	**274%**	**272%**	**Value Gap**	**2,258%**	**3,631%**	**4,371%**
Hotels				**Auctions**			
Marriott International	$9,500	$10,139	$10,242	eBay	$18,800	$8,824	$10,248
Starwood Hotels & Resorts	$6,040	$7,121	$7,050	Priceline	$3,400	$220	$451
Value Gap	**157%**	**142%**	**145%**	**Value Gap**	**553%**	**4,006%**	**2,272%**
Imaging				**Search Engines**			
Eastman Kodak	$18,100	$11,819	$13,508	Yahoo	$60,000	$16,788	$13,297
Xerox	$10,800	$3,085	$4,029	Lycos	$7,700	Acquired	Acquired
Value Gap	**168%**	**383%**	**335%**	**Value Gap**	**779%**	**NA**	**NA**
Health Care				**Semiconductors**			
Pfizer	$278,620	$290,216	$283,907	Intel	$304,600	$202,321	$192,226
Merck	$166,600	$215,125	$184,278	Texas Instruments	$84,200	$82,056	$51,182
Value Gap	**167%**	**135%**	**154%**	**Value Gap**	**362%**	**247%**	**376%**
Basic Materials				**Data Storage**			
Du Pont	$40,900	$50,170	$45,370	EMC	$220,900	$145,503	$86,996
Alcoa	$20,700	$28,976	$30,931	Seagate Technology	$14,600	Acquired	Acquired
Value Gap	**198%**	**173%**	**147%**	**Value Gap**	**1,513%**	**NA**	**NA**

Automobiles				Networking			
Ford Motor	$53,400	$43,453	$51,560	Cisco Systems	$400,400	$275,018	$170,313
General Motors	$35,800	$28,799	$30,146	Network Appliance	$41,000	$20,594	$9,545
Value Gap	**149%**	**151%**	**171%**	**Value Gap**	**977%**	**1,335%**	**1,784%**

Retailing				Online Bookselling			
Wal-Mart	$220,800	$237,292	$223,735	Amazon.com	$14,300	$5,558	$3,638
Home Depot	$126,200	$105,907	$98,518	Barnesandnoble.com	$700	$41	$43
Value Gap	**175%**	**224%**	**227%**	**Value Gap**	**2,043%**	**13,543%**	**8,462%**
Sector Average	175%	212%	207%	Sector Average	1,212%	4,552%	3,453%

Source: Lazard Asset Management, Spencer Stuart analysis.

*Number one and two companies within each sector ranked by market value were selected based on values on September 26, 2000, and updated on December 31, 2000, and February 28, 2001.

Start with the "winner-take-all" phenomenon. In markets such as online search engines and data storage, the first company to establish a solid beachhead has the chance to set the de facto market standard, since it now offers, ostensibly, the solution that's easiest to use, support, and augment.

This is especially true in the technology sector where it's widely known that the brunt of the hardware and software costs are spent up front to build complicated digital products. With the heavy lifting behind them, software and digital infrastructure companies typically incur negligible marginal costs. For example, it costs a fortune to write the computer code underneath Microsoft Word. But once that cost is covered, there's virtually no cost to make another copy of the program. And that's one reason why companies like Microsoft have been such an attractive investment over the long term.

But there's another reason why first is best. AOL, Cisco, and EMC might soar above their nearest competitors, but by contrast, the mountain of dot.com bankruptcies shows that leadership spots fill up quickly. Many of these dead dot.coms—eToys, Pets.com, and Boo.com just to name a few—failed to capitalize on very real opportunities including their high market capitalizations when they had the lead and instead ended up washed against the rocks.

> **"You've read Darwin. He didn't say that the big animals are the ones that survive. He said, it's the ones that adapt and move fastest that survive. And that's true everywhere, even in business." —*Tim Koogle, former CEO, Yahoo!***

It takes courage to move fast and make decisions, especially when the answers are not clear. On the simplest level, you may be wrong and let your team down. At the extreme, a series of bad decisions can cost you your job. A key to executing the go for speed principle is making decisions before all the risk can be taken out of them. If there is no more risk, then you will, by definition, be too late. The Next Economy is so competitive that if you study an issue for too long, competitors will pass you on all sides.

But don't confuse speed and decisiveness with seat-of-the-pants decision-making. It is still vital that companies research, plan, and analyze. While the two concepts—speed on the one hand, and research and analysis on the other—may seem antithetical, they do not have to be. The solution to the seeming paradox lies in changing the traditional strategy development process.

THE WAY IT USED TO BE

Taught in business schools and supported by management consultants of all stripes, strategic planning has been an important management tool for decades. It is the process by which companies set performance objectives, assess challenges and opportunities, and develop business plans. Typically, the process involves an annual planning cycle from which capital is allocated, budgets are constructed, organizational charts are designed, and agreed-upon objectives are committed to.

One of the major traditional economy firms known for its rigorous strategic planning process is Emerson Electric, the St. Louis–based electrical products and electronics equipment manufacturer that until 2001 produced a record 43 consecutive years of increasing earnings per share. Chuck Knight, CEO of Emerson from 1974 to 2000, credits "The Management Process," as it is known, for the company's success. Operating as the equivalent to the spinal cord for the organization, this annual process provides the framework for the top management team meeting with every business unit in the company, and jointly commits to goals, plans, and budgets for the coming year. By the end of the process, everyone has signed off on the strategy and tactics Emerson Electric will deploy over the next 12 months.

This approach has proven itself over time for Emerson Electric. However, whether this same approach will continue to work going forward for companies aiming to thrive in the Next Economy is unclear. Increasingly, businesses using the power of the Internet are becoming more integrated and developing closer ties with their customers than ever before. Web sites are linked, traffic moves fluidly from Web site to Web site, and corporate business development teams negotiate ferociously for the best placements on highly trafficked sites.

In this world of fluid motion, a supplier can become a competitor or a marketing partner overnight. And long-standing rivals can compete in one part of their business while partnering in another. There is even a term for this phenomenon, "coopetition." In long-established companies, the competitive landscape changes so quickly that it reduces the effectiveness of a traditional annual planning cycle.

In today's leading companies, major decisions are often evaluated as scenarios and approached from different angles. Should we build

Relationships are much more fluid and multidimensional in the Next Economy. As a result, rather than manage via a detailed annual strategic planning process, the best leaders will manage via a strategic framework, or business model. It contains most of the elements of a typical business plan, but it allows them to move faster. While the framework is fixed, there is a lot of room for improvisation, something that is critical in today's business environment.

or buy? Acquire or enter into a joint venture? License or sell? Tom Evans, formerly chief executive officer of GeoCities (which was acquired by Yahoo! for $4.5 billion in mid-1999), and who is now CEO of Official Payments Corporation, explains how his company approaches this maze of options. "Each alternative needs to be put through our business model," Evans says. "Going for speed is not to be confused with making it up as you go. People can't just go off creating deals without an understanding of how they fit into the whole of what we are trying to do. This requires us to be incredibly decisive in a short amount of time without having all the information we'd like. The key is to create a rapid, analytical decision-making process that prioritizes our choices to come up with the right answers."

ORGANIZING FOR SPEED

There's an additional way to put the success factor, go for speed, into practice. That is by making sure that the company's values are fully understood, and bought-into by everyone. A company's strong value system can be a sustainable competitive advantage and speed up decision-making. When teams truly understand the company's core values—or as Ronald A. Heifetz, director of the Leadership

Education Project at Harvard University's John F. Kennedy School of Government, puts it, when they know "what is precious and what is not"—they can simply reject out-of-hand proposals or business opportunities once they determine that what is being offered is contrary to the company's values.

What is the best way to structure a company to achieve the speed and flexibility that are required for success in the Next Economy? And, perhaps, more important, can you organize for speed? After all, by definition, flexibility and structure seem antithetical.

But speed and flexibility do not have to be, according to Gary Reiner, General Electric's chief information officer. Listen to how he reconciles speed and bureaucracy: "We have a rule of thumb that says there should be no more than four layers between the CEO of one of our businesses and the shop floor operator. The by-product of this structure is that a lot of us have 30 direct reports. But that's okay, because this kind of arrangement yields a tremendous amount of flexibility that you wouldn't have if you had layers upon layers where everybody has their own little fiefdom. The way we are set up forces everyone to be far more flexible in terms of what they do on a daily basis. When you have four layers, it's so much easier to change than when you've got ten. It's as simple as that."

In talking with dozens of leaders who have built companies that respond quickly and are flexible, certain common characteristics became clear. The starting points in creating a sense of urgency and speed in an organization are to:

- Make the commitment that the organization will act and respond faster. It must become one of the organization's top goals.
- Establish speed and flexibility as key criteria in your hiring process. For example, Yahoo! generally recruits people along two principal criteria, intelligence and an intangible factor that the company calls "proactive behavior." (I'll go into more detail on how that works in chapter 6.)

- Build performance measurements that quantify speed and evaluate *and reward* people against these benchmarks.
- Review the company's entire value chain or business system and look for ways to use technology and good old-fashioned communication to streamline the organization and eliminate bottlenecks. But be careful not to just automate existing processes. As GE's Gary Reiner explains, "It was essential that our Web activities reflect our customers' needs, and not our organizational structure." That is a key distinction. The reason a company must move faster is to meet the needs of its customers, and not to satisfy internal politics.

CREATING A CULTURE TO DO ALL THIS

How can a company create this kind of operating environment—one where everyone is committed to responding to a customer's needs as quickly as possible? Like all major change initiatives, it must start at the top.

"The leader has to have a sense of urgency about this and create a mantra," says Ted Lewis, author of *The Friction-Free Economy* and Kodak's head of Digital Ventures. Lewis, who previously was the North American CEO of Research, Technology, and Ventures at auto giant DaimlerChrysler adds, "It is important that he or she deliver a consistent, clear message to the employees about what they are trying to accomplish. And the message has to be repeated continually. For example, when I first tried to modify the DaimlerChrysler R&D business model, I found myself saying over-and-over again: 'We have to move fast; be innovative, and take responsibility for technology transfer to all parts of the company.' At first the mantra doesn't have much meaning. And after a while it has many meanings. But after an even longer period of time—if you are consistent in what you say—people start to get it. Once everyone knows what you mean by the mantra, you can start to move forward quickly."

The next step along the road to increased speed and flexibility, as practiced by winning companies, is to remove the organizational impediments to change. That, too, is part of the leadership culture, and it is something that the next two companies you are about to meet understand.

Akamai Technologies, the Cambridge, Massachusetts-based, software company that makes up our first case study, is a service provider to firms that do business on the Web. Its entire business, which likes to describe itself as the "FedEx of the Web," is centered on helping its customers get information faster to *their* end-users. Commerce One is a software firm that helps *Fortune* 1000 companies move their businesses to the Internet to the fullest and fastest extent possible.

As you will see in the Akamai story, and in the Commerce One case study that follows it, a key trait of the organization is, in the words of Akamai chairman George Conrades, the fact that "We revere speed."

Let's take a look at how both firms do just that.

10 Ways to Go for Speed[1]

1. Be first to market—or a smart and fast follower.
2. Set up simple but executable business modules.
3. Show people the corporate map.
4. Flatten the company.
5. Share the vision.
6. Measure and reward speed.
7. Let technology aid communications—not take it over.
8. Analyze your company's path of decision-making.
9. Think 24/7.
10. Lead by example.

1. Each of the 10 ways to Go for Speed—and execute the other success factors—is elaborated on in chapter 10.

CASE STUDY

Akamai Technologies
"We Revere Speed"

George Conrades loves to go fast. The 61-year-old CEO of Akamai Technologies spends his spare moments humming around a track on a motorcycle. It's an appropriate hobby for someone whose entire venture circles around speed.

To explain its business in simple terms, Akamai (pronounced AH-kum-my; it means intelligent, clever, and informally "cool" in Hawaiian) is responsible for making sure that Web content gets delivered to end-users as quickly as possible. The company (www.akamai.com) does that by intelligently replicating material provided by its customers on its own network, or "farm" of computer servers, and then routing the material to end-users based on a series of proprietary mathematical models that ensure that it arrives as quickly as possible.

Akamai's software allows its customers' content to avoid congestion on the Web. It works so well that some of the sites with the greatest traffic, such as Lycos, CNN.com, and Barnesandnoble.com, among hundreds of others, have become "Akamaized" in the company's marketing parlance.

Akamai's success earned it a meteoric market valuation initially and a healthy one thereafter. Its high point came in early 2000 when it exceeded $20 billion in market value based on 1999 revenues of just $4 million. Following the sober (and somber) market sentiment that emerged after the dot.com crash, Akamai's stock has fallen dramatically, but still supports a valuation of more than a billion dollars on 2000 revenues of $89 million. But this admirable market cap should not be surprising. Akamai's technology pedigree is virtually perfect. The company was started in direct response to a question that Tim Berners-Lee, the man credited with creating the World Wide Web, asked of a colleague at Massachusetts Institute of Technology.

Back in the days when very few people knew what the Internet was, Berners-Lee wondered if there was a way to avoid a problem that he saw as inevitable. Once the Internet became ubiquitous, people would use it as a source of information. But if everyone went to the same Web site—say NASA's—in response to breaking news—like the latest pictures from Jupiter—the site would crash. Berners-Lee asked Tom Leighton, Akamai's cofounder and now chief scientist, but then a professor of applied mathematics at MIT, if something could be done.

Leighton, with the help of Daniel Lewin[1], then an MIT grad student and now Akamai's chief technology officer, got to work in 1995 on creating the algorithms that today are now at the heart of Akamai Technologies. The formulas they developed make sure that requests for information are rerouted around bottlenecks literally faster than in a blink of an eye.

Given that, perhaps we should have expected that Conrades, who joined the company's board in November 1998 and became chairman and CEO in April 1999, would race motorcycles as a hobby and that the company defines long-term planning as looking out further than 90 days.

There is no clearer example of the principle that speed matters than what Akamai does for a living.

1. Danny Lewin, Akamai's cofounder, was a victim on the September 11, 2001, terrorist attack dooming American Airlines Flight 11 from Boston to Los Angeles. Described as the "heart and soul of the company," he was on the way to California to meet customers. According to Akamai executives, "he would have wanted us to keep information flowing across the Internet at a time like this," which is exactly what the company was able to do for its customers.

One way to think about the need for speed is to picture what would happen if we retold the fable of the "Tortoise and the Hare" today. You remember the original story, of course. Overcome by pride, the hare failed to move as quickly as he should have at the end of their historic race, and so the tortoise was able to pass him at the finish line. The moral we were all taught: Slow but steady wins the race.

This allegory doesn't hold up so well to the pressures of the Next Economy. Individuals and companies have come to expect instant gratification and the best-performing organizations are delivering it 24/7. And because they are, speed and flexibility are more than nice traits for an organization to have today. They are necessities. That is a given at Akamai, located in an office building adjacent to the MIT campus in Cambridge, where the company got its start.

"Today you have to shift to an organizational culture from one that makes and sells, to one that senses and responds," says Chairman and CEO George Conrades. This very shift will make things go faster, he adds.

"In the old make-and-sell environment, everything occurs sequentially. You made it and then you sold it," says Conrades, who might be describing the operating environment where he spent the first 30 years of his career—IBM.

"If you are in a sense-and-respond organization, the feedback is continuous, and so is the change process."

> A sense-and-respond organization has a very active feedback loop between the company and its customers. The organization gets immediate feedback, learns from it, and adapts. This is a key to achieving speed.

Conrades gives an example:
"We have institutional memory about every customer and every

interaction we have had with them, because we learn from each of those interactions. And after you see two or three times that some vendor's software in the Web site is causing a problem with content delivery, you recognize that you can either change the service, or understand that it's an opportunity for a new functionality."

What Conrades is talking about is really another way of describing the very active interaction between Akamai and its customers. But this active feedback loop works only if everyone is committed to moving rapidly, something that Conrades understands. He has worked hard to put that kind of culture in place.

"We revere speed," Conrades says. "We revere people who get things done. We celebrate what they do. It's just amazing how people can produce, especially if they realize the culture encourages it and expects it."

But both those elements are critical. The company has to:

- Decide that a fast response time is essential, and then
- Have people in place that can make that commitment a reality.

That puts a tremendous amount of pressure on hiring people who can thrive in a rapidly changing environment. Akamai gets 700 résumés a week, but invites only a handful of candidates in for interviews. What is Akamai looking for in a potential hire?

"We look for employees who," as Conrades says, "just love to pack as much stuff as they can into one day. When you sign up for a company like this, you better bring enormous energy to the job. You better bring very good reflexes. And you better be prepared to push it to the edge. It's extremely intense.

"Great employees are also people who have a tremendous ambition. They really want to do something. They want to effect change. Great employees are people who combine that ambition with being very smart. And so we place a premium on intelligence. It's not that we are looking for good grades. We want to know if they can think."

"God, I love smart people!" Conrades exclaims. "And smart people love other smart people. Trust me, they have no tolerance for anything less. So, ambition and smarts, and energy, are the factors that we look for!" Conrades said, pounding his conference table. This theme is echoed by former Yahoo! CEO Tim Koogle in chapter 6.

And, indeed, those factors are built into the Akamai culture.

"I don't know how our culture exactly got started, but I do know our company was founded by very smart people who attracted other smart people. And we pride ourselves on attracting *only* smart people, people who have an enormous self-confidence in their ability to interact with others and argue. And when I say, argue, I don't mean shout, scream, and yell, 'my way, not yours!' I mean, people who know how to debate and how to learn from each other."

Akamai has an expression that members of the management team use when someone accomplishes an important goal, closes a major new account, or solves a vexing problem. "You're a Titan!" they say. At Akamai, there is no greater compliment.

ORGANIZING FOR SPEED

All the compliments in the world won't help if the company's organizational structure gets in the way. Silos, fiefdoms, and bureaucracies can negate the best intentions.

Akamai has a way to mitigate the bureaucratic nightmare: The company allows the various "disciplines" needed to solve a customer's problem to work together as one team. Conrades uses the way the company handles customer service as an example to show how this works in practice.

There are a number of capabilities that are required to provide service to the customer, he explains. First is the technical know-how.

"Everyone who deals with the customer must be comfortable in understanding what we do, and how our services work," he says. "Then we have to have people who can integrate what we have with the customer's technical requirements. And finally, we need people to manage the account, handle the billing, and so on." At Akamai, all these people work together, instead of being segregated into separate functional groups.

That makes service, from the customer's point of view, faster and more efficient in a general sense. And the company makes sure that this same speed is present when customers have a specific problem.

We have all experienced the maddening way in which most companies handle customer service. After you get through a frustrating phone tree—"Push 1 for this, push 2 for that"—you end up talking with someone who usually knows very little about what you are asking. He then bounces you to someone who knows a bit more. And if that second person can't handle a technical problem—and he often can't—you are finally shifted to the person you should have been talking to in the first place.

From a cost-saving perspective, that may seem to make sense. Having lower-level people do the initial screening saves money in the short term. After all, you do not want to have one of your technical experts spending time giving out the company's mailing address. But from the customers' point of view, it is a waste of their time and money if they can't get to the expert they need immediately.

Akamai understands this, so its customer service is handled in a way that reinforces the company's commitment to speed.

Conrades explains both components:

"Our customer care is closely tied to our research and development unit. In fact, we frequently rotate R&D people through customer care," he says. This, obviously, is part of the Akamai "active feedback loop" cited earlier.

To make this a richer feedback loop, Akamai has experts handle *all* the customer phone calls into the company. The goal? Akamai wants to answer every customer question on the first call, or through the first e-mail.

Conrades first described his customer-care approach in an interview he did for the *Harvard Business Review,* where he explained the customer-care approach in greater detail.

> We looked at that conventional way of handling customer inquiries, and we immediately said, "No way." We need to maintain trust, and we need to build our brand, and in the Internet space, you don't do that by making the customer wait for an answer. On the Internet, a technical problem is a business problem. So everyone in our customer care unit is an expert. It's our responsibility to get the right answer and to get it fast. It's a complex world out there, and the one thing we never want to say is, "Well, that's not our problem." We don't do that. We say, "Whatever it is, we'll help." In fact, we like questions that aren't about our network because they help us learn more about the customer's needs and experiences—all that information is incredibly valuable to our R&D efforts.

"I can't say enough about customer care, because it really is the place where we earn the customer's trust every minute of the day. We've got people who just eat, sleep, and drink customer care. They love it. They love the challenge of solving customers' problems. And they love the technical side of it; they cherish the links to R&D. I sometimes see e-mails with a time stamp of three in the morning with Yahoo or The Motley Fool, for example, demonstrating just how engaged our people are with solving the customer's problem. It never stops. And remember, all those interactions are captured in our database, stored in our institutional memory. So the next time the customer calls, or another customer calls with a similar problem, the information is all there."

Akamai also illustrates one other component of the speed success factor, hard work and long hours.

"You know, we don't have fixed work hours here," Conrades said. "Well, I'm sure we do, because there's probably a legality. But people work their tail off and fly red-eyes to make sure things get done and get done quickly. If you just put in your eight hours and go home, nothing is getting done; things just drag on and on."

We've delved deeply into how Akamai follows the speed principle. But as you can probably tell, the company is one of the great players of the Next Economy, embracing, in fact, all six of the factors for success. Akamai obsesses the customer, goes for speed, is a learning organization. But more important, the company also does a masterful job of "absorbing uncertainty"—a phrase that Conrades coined and which best describes our fifth success factor. Part of the company's accomplishment is in how the company abides by its Statement of Purpose and lives by its Governing Principles, which follow:

Akamai Statement of Purpose[2]

Akamai exists to profitably provide businesses and organizations with:

—A dependable, high-performance platform for the creation and delivery of engaging, interactive Web content, streaming media, and Internet applications,

—through services that are scalable, easily implemented, and easily managed,

—while capitalizing on innovative technology and collaborative relationships both inside and outside the company,

—which result in superior customer satisfaction, attractive shareholder returns and a desirable place to work.

2. Reprinted with permission.

Akamai Governing Principles (Part I)

We will always . . .

1. Work closely with customers to understand and anticipate their needs.
2. Respond to customers with world-class service based on innovative technology.
3. Pursue innovation to continually improve customers' value.
4. Maintain the security of customers' information and ensure their trust in us.
5. Deliver on our commitments to all stakeholders.
6. Encourage employee innovation, initiative, and appropriate risk-taking.
7. Foster a work environment that attracts, motivates, and retains high caliber employees.
8. Respect employees, customers, and business partners.
9. Communicate openly and honestly.
10. Work cooperatively for the sake of our customers and ahead of internal differences.
11. Measure our progress.
12. Conduct our business with the highest level of ethics and integrity.
13 Strive for excellence in all we do.
14. Have fun.

Akamai Governing Principles (Part II)

We will never . . .

1. Ignore profit.
2. Dismiss ideas from any source without consideration.
3. Promise what we cannot deliver.
4. Violate the trust of customers, their clients, business partners, employees, or shareholders.
5. Allow any abuse in the work environment including harassment or discrimination of any kind.
6. Veer from our Statement of Purpose and Governing Principles.

LEARNING TO BE QUICK

Many managers think that they cannot teach people to react quickly.

Many managers would be wrong, says Yobie Benjamin, Distinguished Fellow at Ernst and Young, where he oversaw the $2 billion global e-commerce practice (up until the time the consulting arm was sold to French consulting company Cap Gemini, in 2000).

"Let's start with a definition," Benjamin says. "A person who moves fast and is flexible must be someone who is highly adaptable. When he or she finds himself or herself in a situation where there are limited tools, this person uses those tools to best advantage. It is clear if you define speed and flexibility this way, then what we are talking about can be learned.

"How is it best learned?" Benjamin asks rhetorically. "By example."

The examples must be set from the top down, says Benjamin. As confirmed in all of the research that went into this book, leading by example is one of the enduring principles of leadership. Top leaders who themselves behave in adaptable ways, who personally and genuinely react to feedback by incorporating it into their words *and* behaviors, will allow speed and flexibility to thrive and reverberate throughout the organization. A company's leadership that talks about speed, adaptability, change, and innovation but does not live by its own words will have no credibility. There is nothing *less* inspiring to an employee than a manager who does not walk the talk.

On the other hand, leaders can inspire employees to act in ways that will truly help the company execute successfully.

"Flexibility can be learned as well," Benjamin adds. But he believes that people are more adaptable than they are given credit for. "I think by nature, human beings are flexible. If you were inflexible, you would have driven through a brick wall this morning as you were pulling out of your garage. We all learn to adjust to the environment around us. Perhaps some adapt better than others, but we all adapt."

Flexible, innovative people can become energized by a company's commitment to speed, and stretch to meet the needs of their customers, according to the leaders we interviewed. Like many characteristics, speed and flexibility are usually seen only in committed employees who engage personally in the company and their jobs. Employees need to feel *accountable* for the company's success or failure—not just *responsible* for their particular job or hours. The payoff can be enormous.

CASE STUDY

Commerce One
"You Still Have to Build a Business"

Mark Hoffman and the people who work at Commerce One have a unique perspective on the changes transpiring in today's turbulent economy. And they, perhaps better than most, understand the vital importance of moving quickly.

For one thing, as a company that sets up huge Web-based trading exchanges, the Pleasanton, California-based, company is at the forefront of the Next Economy and Web marketplaces. For another, Commerce One's 3,500 employees get to see both sides of the economy's technology-driven transformation, since a large proportion of its customers are Fortune 100 companies. One of Commerce One's landmark achievements, for example, was its role in setting up Covisint, the global automotive business-to-business purchasing exchange for General Motors (see chapter 7), Daimler-Chrysler, Ford, Nissan, and Renault in 2000. Analysts say this combination has the potential of being the first trillion-dollar enterprise in corporate history. GM became a significant investor in Commerce One as a result of the deal.

Commerce One has changed a tremendous amount in a short time. Founded in 1994 as Distri Vision, the company was reborn in

1997 as Commerce One and went public in 1999. In 2000 it reported revenues of $400 million and in June 2001 had a $1.2 billion inmarket capitalization (down from a high of over $16 billion in September 2000). The company has developed the "Commerce One Solution" to automate the procurement cycle between multiple buyers and suppliers. In July 2000 the company formed Commerce One Ventures to accelerate global participation in e-business through strategic investments.

Since the Internet moves at remarkable speed, winning companies need to respond quickly. But what sometimes gets overlooked, amid all the attention given to the sophisticated technology that underpins a company such as Commerce One, is the fact that Internet-based firms still have to (quickly) build a business. Technology is all well and good. But at some point (and sooner than later of late) you have to create a real, economically viable business around it.

Hoffman is a 54-year-old West Point–trained engineer, and the founder and former CEO of Sybase, one of the largest independent software companies in the world. He explains Commerce One's past, so that we can get a firm handle on its future. You may be surprised at how quickly it all came together.

Commerce One's evolution, which is all about speed, is also rooted in customer obsession and learning, two of our core success factors, elaborated upon in the coming chapters.

"Initially, we focused on selling software to companies that bought from our customers. Our goal was to make all of our customers doing business together easier," Hoffman explains. After all, if Commerce One's products were the common thread across various companies, it would strengthen its bonds with these customers.

"And then as we really began to understand our customers more and more deeply and see how technology was transforming their businesses, we saw new patterns emerge around fusing buyers and suppliers more closely together. That evolved into the whole concept of marketplaces, and the creation of Internet-based market sites, where you have a centralized facility for all inter-company transactions and communications.

"That then expanded from creating stand alone market sites into integrated communities where market sites themselves could communicate with one another. As a result, we began to create something we called the Global Trading Web, which is a network of interoperable marketplaces, trading communities and commerce portals that have the ability for market-site-to-market-site communication."

Responding to clients' needs is what drove all these changes. The more Commerce One did, the more its clients wanted it to do. And this customer obsession and learning led to the company's executing against two of our other success factors, risk-taking and speed.

Building quickly off its success, Commerce One took a major step. Working directly with General Motors, it created the world's largest online commercial marketplace, a clearinghouse where GM, DaimlerChrysler, Ford, Nissan, and Renault could buy all their component parts through the same central facility. It was a major risk trying to bring archrivals together into an alliance, involving countless team-member hours and millions of dollars in development work—and the venture still has many hurdles to clear. But for Commerce One, the brave new partnership has already paid huge dividends.

"It was a great thing for GM, and a great thing for Commerce One," Hoffman says. "The creation of that exchange got everybody else in the marketplace moving. The aerospace companies, the oil and gas companies, the utilities, and others all started to come together as a result of what they saw us do with the automotive industry. The catalyst was our work for GM, Ford and DaimlerChrysler (which were the three founding members of the exchange). It was an unbelievable accelerator." Nissan and Renault joined the alliance after its establishment by the Big Three.

How do you create a joint venture of this size and scope? Very carefully, says Hoffman. In fact, the story of how the joint venture initially came together demonstrates the obstacles that must be overcome—and the important role of a third party like Commerce One.

As a General Motors executive told me the story, on a quiet Sunday afternoon in January 2000, Harold Kutner, GM's group vice president for worldwide purchasing, got a surreptitious phone call at home. The caller wanted to know if he would consider joining forces with archrival Ford Motor Company to build a common integrated supplier exchange on the Internet. The idea of teaming up with Ford, of all companies, seemed nothing less than an unnatural act to Kutner. "Are you kidding?" Kutner is reported to have said. "I wouldn't waste five minutes discussing this." But the caller persisted, making an interesting case that both GM and Ford had both already launched online trade exchanges as part of their e-business initiatives. In so doing, they had thrown their vast supplier networks into a panic, for if every car maker built its own online exchange, suppliers would be forced to create technical links to each one, adding complexity and costly technological implementations. Why not build a single common exchange that would benefit all those involved? So a secret, late-night meeting was set up. When Kutner arrived, he found Brian Kelley, his counterpart at Ford, along with Ray Lane, then chief operating officer of Oracle, Ford's software partner, and Hoffman. Through Commerce One's catalytic efforts, the group agreed to set up teams from each company to explore the benefits of the group effort and soon concluded that the venture made sense and the unprecedented cooperative agreement began. The third giant automaker, DaimlerChrysler, was quickly brought into the mix. By February, the trio announced the formation of Covisint, the world's largest virtual marketplace.

Hoffman cites the three key factors required to make such ventures work, beginning with the need to pay a lot of attention to the deal, not only during the negotiations but after. And that can take enormous and intensive time commitment, something often at odds with the way business has to be done today.

"You have to move it along, but you can't be impatient. You have to be very persistent, because in the process of creating a fair deal you are going to have up and downs. In the case of the Ford-GM-Chrysler marketplace, it was more than a year after we started working that we had actually had a signed final contract."

Not surprisingly, if a deal is to work, the CEO has to be the driver. Hoffman says that overall deal-making and acquisitions take about 15% to 20% of his time, and that it requires virtually 100% when things heat up.

"For a deal like the one we did with GM, or any of our key deals, I make many red eye trips," Hoffman recalls. "There was one month where I flew out to Detroit six times. We'd fly out of here at eight o'clock at night, get an hour's sleep, and be in to see GM the next morning. At those moments, the deal has to be the CEO's top priority.

"You've got to manage the relationship just like every other piece of your business," he explains. "We're dedicating lots of people to making sure that the relationship really works. We're working to build product jointly. And we've got joint go-to-market strategies that we're working on as well."

But a major time and people commitment is just one factor.

"You've got to have creative people," Hoffman adds. "You've got to have great people in the business development area who are very creative. And that's got to be driven from the CEO down.

"I think you need people who really can understand the market and a business. People who know where the markets are going and who can get very creative around the deal structure."

And perhaps most important, the deal has to work for everyone.

"You've got to create a win-win," is the way Hoffman puts it. "I think we're pretty tough negotiators. But the goal is not to take every penny off the table for you or your people. It's to create what is in the end a fair deal."

"HERE'S WHAT I THINK YOU SHOULD DO"

Given the high-profile initial success of those early deals, Hoffman finds himself consulting with *Fortune* 100 companies about how they could best use the Internet to smooth out the supply chain. It's still unclear how much electronic commerce will ultimately help companies gain greater cost efficiencies—and that forces Commerce One to absorb a fair amount of uncertainty.

But what's crystal clear is that Hoffman is preaching to CEOs about the inevitable future technological forces that will shape their profit-and-loss statements for years and years to come. So it's worth tuning into his unorthodox pitch: "I think it has become clear to everyone that large companies, one have to move more quickly, and two have to be more aggressive," Hoffman says. "They need to change the way that they manage their supply chains today in the marketplace. As it is structured, it's way too rigid and inflexible." One way to move faster while minimizing potential risks, Hoffman believes, is for large firms to consider teaming up with traditional rivals, so they both can benefit.

"Electronic commerce is going to continue to allow established companies to be much more flexible," he says. "For example, in the case of the automotive exchange, it is ultimately going to change the way the major auto companies build their cars," by changing their sourcing strategies, reducing costs, and accelerating the time from order to sale.

What is the best way to organize a new marketplace exchange? Hoffman's experience to date of building and implementing scores of these new marketplace businesses has convinced him that organizing them as an independent entity is the best way to go. Doing so brings the advantages of the incumbent organizations in terms of scale, resources, financial muscle, and management depth while addressing their traditional weaknesses such as inability to move quickly and intolerance for risk.

"In a lot of cases, our clients are committing independent management to develop their marketplaces and incorporating them as new companies. I think that is the right choice," he says. "You've got to treat it like you're creating your own little company or at least division. You can't cautiously invest thinking it's going to be profitable in six months. It really needs to be treated as a startup company. It's no different than other early-stage, venture-backed companies. You've got to go through a period with no profitability within that company before you end up where you want to be by reaching the required size.

"The hard part is not the technology in building these exchanges. It's the business practices around the exchange. You can get the technology up and running in a matter of days or weeks. But the question is what kind of a business are you going to run once you create it.

"What I always tell clients is that it's not the technology that you need to focus on in building an exchange, it's really creating the business around the e-marketplace. They have to know: who are going to be the buyers and the suppliers within that exchange, and what it is exactly that the exchange is going to offer."

"Companies now have an opportunity to revolutionize both how they procure goods and how they transact and interact with their trading community. This is a vision not only of revolutionizing procurement within the four walls of an enterprise, but also extending the solution beyond the enterprise, to interact electronically with suppliers, customers, and distributors. In short, it is a vision of completely integrated, end-to-end commerce solutions, solutions that tie corporate intranets and extranets together. But companies need to treat this idea as a business." —Mark Hoffman, CEO, Commerce One

Commerce One, along with its archrivals Oracle, Ariba, and their customers, have essentially created a new industry in building automated marketplace exchanges. They could not have been created on a large scale before the advent of the Internet. In creating a new industry, companies and individuals are bound to be bounced around quite a bit. Commerce One has experienced this firsthand. It has seen its stock trade anywhere between $84 and $5.00 a share, between September 2000 and April 2001, due to general market conditions and the specific outlook for e-marketplaces and Commerce One at any given moment. On top of that, when a company is moving as quickly as Commerce One, some employees are going to feel uncomfortable.

In situations like this, it is incumbent upon the leadership to be a stabilizing influence. Hoffman understands that. He deals with the question of the company's stock price first.

"I am pretty philosophical about how others outside the company react to us," Hoffman says. "Maybe it is because I've had quite a bit of experience with a lot of ups and downs at the other places I've worked. But I try to get people to ignore what others are saying about us. What I tell them is, 'Hey, we're building a major company in the B-to-B space. And we're going to be a significant player over time. And when I say over time, I am not talking about six or nine months. That is not our battleground. I'm talking about years and years of building this company.'

"And I tell them there will be ups and downs and all kinds of market gyrations in between. But that doesn't matter. You really just have to focus on executing against the business plan. We've been exceeding all of our business plan projections all along. That was true when the stock was at $150, and it was also true when it was at $30. So I just encourage our people to keep their heads down, and execute. Eventually, the stock price will go back up as long as we deliver. That's what has happened in the past and what will continue to happen."

The message seems to be working.

"I think people like the space we're in. We are able to hire at a phenomenal rate here because engineers are excited about building products in this area. People are energized because they feel that we're just in the first or second inning. They like the idea of being part of a growth company. So people continue to be very positive and excited."

That is not surprising. Winning in the Next Economy will be a consequence when you focus on all of the 6 factors for success, especially the one that calls for you to assume a leadership position very quickly.

CHAPTER 4

Success Factor #2
Create a Learning Organization

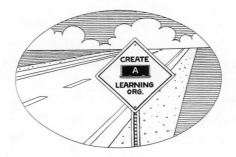

Introduction

The notion of a "learning organization" has become quite "in" these days. Scores of executives blithely bandy the term about to describe their companies. But take a hard look at most corporations and you'll find that they aren't really learning organizations in the truest sense of the words.

Then again, the words themselves have taken on different meanings over the years. The term, as some might remember, first came into fashion in the late 1980s, and like many business buzzwords, it has been overused, misused, and misappropriated ever since. Today, companies that offer "on-the-job training" consider themselves learning organizations. But that's only part of the equation. For our purposes, we're thinking of the term in a different—and more fundamental—context.

Becoming a learning organization in the Next Economy will be a direct result of what people take away from their interactions with colleagues, partners, suppliers, customers, investors, and any other stakeholders in the corporation. The knowledge from these interactions will become the lifeblood of any growing, healthy organization. Employees on the front lines dealing with customers, for example, will garner the critical bits of information about what is working and what is not and how the organization is being perceived from different vantage points. One of the keys to success in the coming years will be not only to capture that information but to act on it in order to create new products and services that are demanded by your customers.

> The learning organization is one that actively looks for insights in all its interactions with others—and then acts on them.

Here's the upshot: To win in the Next Economy, companies must capture the learning that takes place every day at companies around the world—but they must also transmit that knowledge to the parts of the organization that need it most. The faster this can be done, the greater impact it can have on creating the best products and services a company has to offer. And it will ultimately separate winning companies from losers. A learning organization is also a seductive lure for the kind of winning employees that business leaders are looking for more than ever these days.

A UNIQUE OPPORTUNITY

The Internet itself is really one big learning opportunity. Using the Web, companies can get feedback in ways that were never possible before. A highly involved online community becomes an avenue for enhancing service and increasing customer satisfaction through immediate feedback loops that can be constructed between customers

and the company. And here's where you can see that a learning organization is one that also obsesses the customer and establishes the
need for speed.

Consider The Motley Fool and its cofounders, Tom and David
Gardner, our first case study in this chapter. For this company, a
leading online community of 2 million members taking control of
their financial destinies, listening to the customer is not just a nice
bromide plastered on the wall in some fancy corporate lobby. It's the
cornerstone of the company's product strategy. This idea is so in-
trinsic to The Motley Fool mission that it's no longer just another
thing they do; it's what they *are*. In other words, The Motley Fool
exists in a constant state of listening and responding to the people
who use their products. And the company has become one of the
best examples of how an organization can fluidly learn, apply, and
transmit knowledge and information from the customer.

"Our community is really our R&D lab," says Tom Gardner. "We
recently noticed that a tremendously vibrant chat area on Fool.com
was the whole area of home ownership. As a result, we are planning
new books, areas on the site, and services for home buying and financing." And as we will see in a moment, listening to their customers also helped create a new business concept that led to an
innovative experiment—publishing reports by their members. As
The Motley Fool case study will demonstrate, creating a learning organization can facilitate lightning-fast product development, a critical competitive differentiator in the Next Economy.

Akamai Technologies has created a learning organization in a
slightly different way. Chairman and CEO George Conrades explained that one of the key things that will separate winners from
the also-rans in the next few years will be, "a culture that senses and
responds, versus makes and sells."

"The sense and respond culture is a collaborative effort,"
Conrades said. "It leads to better products and services for customers
and a better work force. In the old make and sell environment,

everything is sequential. The company makes the product and then they scream at the sales force to push it—'I don't want to hear your concerns, just sell that stuff,' they say. In our environment, we get 50 to 60 requests a week for changes and we are releasing new products and services that incorporate this feedback."

Most companies that listen to their customers learn what they like and what they don't about the company's products. But in strong learning organizations, companies not only learn how to make their existing products better, their customers can actually help develop new ones.

As you'll see more clearly, that's precisely what is happening at The Motley Fool and eBay, the world's leading online marketplace.

Let's first take a closer look at The Motley Fool.

---

10 Ways to Create a Learning Organization

1. Shorten feedback cycles.
2. Transfer knowledge.
3. Expand the company's "listening circles."
4. Focus on what is really going on rather than just on appearances.
5. Measure the right things to support learning.
6. Reward teaching and learning.
7. Study and remember history.
8. Encourage employees' activities outside of their jobs.
9. Assess each learning initiative in the context of your organizational culture to ensure effectiveness.
10. Acknowledge others' efforts to change.

CASE STUDY
The Motley Fool
Teach and Learn

It all started, as the founders of The Motley Fool are fond of saying, with chocolate pudding.

When they were young, brothers David and Tom Gardner learned about the stock market and the business world from their father, a banker and economist. To his credit, Dad would present ideas about supply and demand, earnings, and share prices in terms that the boys could not only understand but also savor.

"See that pudding?" their father asked one day during a trip to the supermarket. "We own [shares in] the company that makes it. Every time someone buys that pudding, it's good for our company—and that means it is good for us. So, go get some more!"

The boys quickly caught on to business in general and to investing specifically. And to the surprise of many of their peers, they found the subjects fun. So why not turn their avocation into a job?

Shortly after graduation, David and Tom, along with college friend Erik Rydholm, founded what they boldly called "the world's premier multimedia financial education company," although firms such as McGraw-Hill (publishers of *Business Week, Standard & Poors*) and AOL Time Warner (with the world's largest online service, CNN, and a host of magazines such as *Fortune*) might quibble. The three friends called their fledgling start-up: The Motley Fool.

Why that name? "In Elizabethan drama, the Fool was the only character who told the King the truth," the Gardners explain. "Everyone else was too consumed with pride, greed, position, and power. In The Motley Fool forum, our readers are our royalty."

The company's mission has remained the same since its inception: "To educate, enrich and amuse individuals around the world."

The company's founders elaborate on the story from there:

The Motley Fool drew its first breath in 1993, when the three friends created a modest 16-page print newsletter, mixing investing information and humor. They borrowed some friends' and relatives' wedding invitation lists and sent out a bunch of sample issues with invitations to subscribe. Even selling to this friendly crowd, they only received a few subscriptions. After publishing 12 monthly issues, it gradually became clear that the publication wasn't catching on.

Something else was, though. The Internet. In the early to mid-1990s Americans in rapidly growing numbers were going online.

Tom Gardner was no exception. While logged onto the Prodigy service, he began answering people's financial questions. Soon the flow of questions and answers took up most of his and David's time. They moved onto America Online, tap-tap-tapping out conversations late into the night with strangers around the nation and world. This flurry of interest and activity did not go unnoticed. Soon America Online invited them to become part of its incubator, the "Greenhouse." With funds from AOL, the brothers were able to move out of the shack behind David's house into the two-room ground floor of a townhouse in Alexandria, Virginia. The money also enabled them to buy more computers, begin hiring employees, and lure another of Tom's old friends, Gary Hill, to balance the books.

By 1994 The Motley Fool was online. Using $50,000 of their own money, the brothers established the "Fool Portfolio" to use as both a teaching tool and an investment. In a little over five years, the portfolio (renamed the "Rule Breaker Portfolio") has grown to more than $450,000 in value, which works out to be about a 40% return each year, at a time when the overall stock market has only done a third as well. The Rule Breaker Portfolio is designed to identify breakthrough, market-creating companies, such as Human Genome Sciences (Nasdaq: HGSI), Celera (NYSE: CRA), and Starbucks (Nasdaq: SBUX). Check the investing strategies section of Fool.com for the current portfolio.

Over time, another handful of portfolios were created, each with a different investing style intended to complement the Rule Breaker Portfolio. The most significant is the "Rule Maker Portfolio." This broad-based portfolio, with companies such as General Electric, Coca-Cola, Intel, and Ford, is constructed to identify the leaders of existing industries. These portfolios are not meant to serve as specific stock recommendations, but instead to teach by example. And teaching and learning from its customers is what the company is still all about. We will see this exemplified first in the way the company went about testing a new service, Soapbox.com, and then later in how they determined that it was time to hire an experienced professional manager to become the company's chief executive officer.

In retrospect, it probably shouldn't be surprising that The Motley Fool tested the publishing business via Soapbox.com, which was designed to be a platform for customers to communicate their ideas to a broader audience. After all, the venture was just a logical offshoot of what the multimedia company had been doing all along.

Building off the company's successful online launch in 1994, The Motley Fool grew remarkably quickly simply by responding to its customers needs. People who visited the site loved reading Tom's and Dave's colorfully written commentary online, but customers constantly asked if there was a way to capture what they were reading— and being taught—in a more permanent form.

So, less than two years after the Fools' beginning Tom and David became traditional authors. The pair struck a deal that led to the publication of four business best-sellers, two of which—*The Motley Fool Investment Guide* and *You Have More Than You Think*—have recently been revised, updated, and reissued to keep pace with continued demand. David's and Tom's success also paved the way for a healthy self-publishing business at The Motley Fool itself, and to date, more than a dozen books by Fool writers and analysts have been published.

From there, a weekly nationally syndicated newspaper feature was added (in 1997) and a nationally syndicated radio show (in 1998). And in 1999 the company launched *The Motley Fool Monthly* magazine. Though the magazine was discontinued after a year, its brief appearance helped lead to a partnership with *Newsweek* magazine, which in 2001 published a series of co-branded Motley Fool features. All of this media was designed to serve their audience's interests *and* to drive traffic to Fool.com. This was and continues to be part of the company's strategy to "attract, addict, and convert" members to the Fool community.

In early 2001, in fact, when the great Internet advertising devaluation occurred—rocking so many dot-com business models and deflating the tech-heavy Nasdaq—The Motley Fool curiously found itself in a stronger-than-ever position. How? The Fool had long ago established itself as much more than an Internet company, and while the online portion of its business was most certainly fighting to stabilize revenues, its offline properties—books, newspaper and magazine columns, radio show, and a well-timed PBS television special—were propelling the brand forward. Indeed, the Fool's online and offline products seemed to be feeding off each other, creating a very real example of "cross-platform synergy." In March 2001 when traffic to such financial Web sites as Marketwatch.com and RagingBull.com was slumping, Fool.com attracted 2.7 million visitors—an all-time high for the company. To be sure, traditional media were driving much of that online interest, and vice versa. All told, an estimated 30 million people were touched by the Fool brand on one platform or another during a single challenging month. More than a dot-com, indeed.

But most of the traditional media was one way—Fool to customers. Nothing wrong with that, of course. It was how the company got started. But about six years after it got under way, it was time to evolve again.

In the same way that AOL noticed that Tom Gardner was handling a lot of questions about personal finance, Motley Fool staffers noticed that there were some community members who were providing expertise of their own to fellow users through the company's bulletin boards and the like. Chat rooms and e-mails back and forth were certainly one way that information could flow, but staffers wondered whether there was a more efficient forum.

After a bit of head scratching, the company came up with a new idea—an experimental new service. It was called Soapbox.com and while it lasted only a year, it is worth examining because the effort proved valuable in its short life. It provided the company with invaluable lessons about how to listen to one's customers and learn.

> **"The Internet really enables you to listen to what people actually want from your service, what they cherish, what they don't like, what they'd like to see you add, what they never want to see you do in terms of different services or products you can offer. Every business needs to listen to its customers. The Internet makes it incredibly easy to do that." —Tom Gardner, co-founder, The Motley Fool**

SOAPBOX STORY

During the summer of 2000, The Motley Fool launched Soapbox.com, as an interactive online marketplace "where people could buy and sell information for education, fun and profit." The first authors posted reports on subjects ranging from biotech to wireless communication to investing in the stock market. Soapbox.com was to be a channel through which any member of the Fool community could become an author. Writers created their own content, determined what they wanted to charge for it, and placed it on Soapbox.com's digital publishing platform—which immediately made it available to an audience of more than 2 million potential readers via Fool.com. Soapbox.com offered built-in distribution, and a platform to enable direct, reader-to-author-to-reader interaction.

David Gardner gives an example of one of the site's first bestsellers. "A report was written by a guy on *Retiring Early*. And he had retired early himself. So in his report, he takes you through his thinking on how he did it, and why his approach differs from conventional wisdom out there, which has it that people retire when they're 65. Just as there was a conventional wisdom 75 years ago that you never retired. And his point is productivity gains and new technologies should allow people to retire a lot earlier than 65 if they start getting a plan together. He thinks they may actually be able to target 50 now. The average kind of middle class worker, as he's defined it, should be thinking about age 50 to 55."

One of the intriguing things about the Soapbox.com model was that consumers could share their evaluations of the articles and books they bought through a public rating system. That way, similar to the popular reader reviews on Amazon.com, there was a built-in feedback loop, giving both the authors and the community the ability to learn from each other. Authors who provided useful information became better known, and those who didn't found it harder to sell their works.

Tom Gardner put the creation of the new service in perspective: "The opportunity we tried to create for people at Soapbox.com was analogous to what David and I established in building The Motley Fool," he explains. "Back in 1994, the Fool was essentially the two of us up on our soapbox, teaching and learning from people about all kinds of financial topics. Similarly, the authors at Soapbox.com were engaged in the same interactive cycle of teaching and learning. In just a few months, we saw many of them build their soapboxes into thriving online communities and businesses."

Recognized by many users, reporters, and industry experts as an innovative business concept, Soapbox.com attracted hundreds of authors and thousands of customers in a very short period of time. It also taught The Motley Fool many critical lessons about entrepreneurism, the strength of the company's community, the challenges of outsourcing technology, and the resource requirements involved in spinning off a sub-brand.

Sounds good. So why didn't it fly? One reason: capital starvation. After carefully examining many different strategic and financial options for the service, the company determined that the investment required to propel Soapbox.com beyond its start-up phase was too large to shoulder alone—but in the frigid capital markets, outside financing wasn't an option. Soapbox, unfortunately, fell upon the heap of Internet experiments. But it was anything but foolish. It was precisely the sort of valuable failed experiment that has become part of the company's growing knowledge base. Had the company taken nothing away from the Soapbox experience, the effort would have been in vain. But that wasn't the case.

The Fool continues to build upon the idea that it is a "community" service and a trusted marketplace of ideas—Soapbox was just one evolutionary strain of that larger principle. The basic concept can sprout into many other diverse directions.

"I think the thing that we benefit most from is having such a vibrant and strong community," says David Gardner. "A lot of the stand-alone, 'expert' sites which have launched in the past year or two are ones that have started up as economic applications but have no basis in learning or education or haven't cultivated any community.

"I think one of the reasons that Soapbox was such a valuable experiment was that it was built on top of what was already a vibrant and strong community at the Fool. That meant there were already potential buyers and potential sellers built in. Obviously, there were not enough to justify further investment in the concept at the time.

But at similar sites, the biggest stumbling block has tended to be that buyers don't have enough information, or don't trust the sellers. We had a leg up on that count because the sellers already had established reputations in the message boards and because The Motley Fool has proven its value and credibility to current and potential customers."

COMING FULL CIRCLE

Despite Soapbox.com's quick departure from the marketplace, the Gardners remain extremely proud that they were able to create a service as a direct result of listening to their customers, and that it served as an exciting reminder of what got them into business in the first place. They have a feeling of accomplishment, yes. But more than that, they have a sense of fulfillment.

"There are a lot of elements that got built into Soapbox," Tom Gardner explains. "For one thing, we extended our teaching and generated a lot of learning. And of course, we learned a lot ourselves. I don't want to overstate this, but there is a natural satisfaction to teaching, to know that you've improved someone's life. We've seen that for years at our book signings. A lot of people come out to tell us, 'You just saved me $1,800 buying my car,' or 'I was able to take early retirement thanks to The Fool.' That is obviously incredibly satisfying. But it's so much more than that.

"Because, as The Motley Fool has shown, our basic business premise was right—people want to learn, to hear the truth, to improve their lives—and as a result of acting on that premise, we were able to hire our friends, people that we love. So now we have something that is incredibly satisfying to do, and people that we love surround us. And then, as it builds, the media begins to get turned on to what we're doing, and everything plays into happiness in the mind. I think happiness is the simplest way to describe what most people are looking for in life. And, obviously, we all find it in different ways.

"So what we are doing is inherently satisfying. We're surrounded by people we love, and we believe we are creating a lot of value. In the end, out of nothing, we've created a fair amount of value and we believe that we're still early on in the process. Not surprisingly, it has not been hard for us to motivate people to come to work every day here, because they feel the same things themselves.

"In fact, a year ago, for the fun of it, we did what we call our happiness index. It sprung up out of the blue. We started hearing from a couple of people, 'It's not the same at the Fool today as it used to be. It's more corporate.' So we decided to see how genuinely felt that was. So we created a single Web page. Everyone comes in and answers: 'Are you happy?' The second question is this, 'If you're happy, why? If you're not happy, what can we do to improve things?'

"From these simple questions, we got a torrent of feedback. And while we found out that the vast majority of people at the company were happy, we had concrete things we could improve. But overall, we were able to confirm in our minds that what we were doing was the right way to build a business." People outside the company seem to agree. *Mademoiselle* magazine, for example, named The Motley Fool one of the top 25 places in America to work.

And what, in summary, was The Motley Fool's company-building philosophy? "Create something you enjoy, work with people you love, and listen to what your customers want so you can both teach and learn."

LEARNING IT'S TIME FOR HELP

Learning is not always easy, and sometimes we learn things about our organizations that we may rather not admit. For the Gardner brothers, they eventually came to grips with the fact that their small company had outgrown their self-taught management style. The Motley Fool eventually became a formidable media corporation with more than 250 employees, nearly 3 million unique visitors per month to the Fool.com, and more than 2 million registered users.

That sort of growth required professional management—especially when you heap on to all of this additional capital-raising in the background.

So the search began. To run an organization like The Motley Fool, it takes a rare individual. The Gardner brothers wanted someone who would clearly be a bright leader and offer a deep marketing and management experience. But they also knew that the person needed to understand their commitment to hearing their customers and leveraging technology to be responsive to the users' needs. The cultural fit was paramount.

After sifting through 17 external candidates over a period of more than 44 weeks, the company chose C. Patrick Garner to help them get to the next level. Pat had spent 30 years at Coca-Cola, most recently running 10 countries in its Southeast Asian operations, before deciding to move into the digital economy.

John Huey, editorial director at Time Inc., describes his long-time friend "as perhaps the best marketing man and general manager I know." As the Gardners got to know Pat and did their due diligence, they became convinced that the senior executive with the last name similar to theirs (and who ironically enough has a striking resemblance to Tom Gardner) was just the right individual to lead The Motley Fool into the future. Pat established an initial management approach of "listen, learn and lead," and that is exactly what he has done, says David Gardner.

"Almost immediately—within the first 60 to 80 days of Pat's being here, we had gained amazing clarity about what we are trying to do as an organization," Gardner says. "Before we all felt good to be working here. But now we are psyched because we are moving toward a common goal."

Pat quickly created a simple but powerful strategic management framework to guide all of the company's activities. First, he created a destination, which he called "5x/3y." This is the concrete objective to achieve a fivefold increase in the company's value in three years.

Then, he established quantifiable performance measures to drive this growth, such as increase revenue by a defined rate per year, achieve positive cash flow by a certain date, increase unique visitors by a certain rate by a certain time. And finally, he distilled six operating imperatives to give the organization the tools to achieve these objectives. They were to:

- Operate like a public company
- Plan, execute, measure, learn
- Deliver operating effectiveness and efficiency
- Establish a budget management process
- Communicate, coordinate, consolidate, and
- Build our project management capability

It turned out that the organization responded beautifully to having a tangible road map for how to operate. For Garner, how was the transition from one of the most prestigious corporations in the world to an early stage Internet company?

Initially, looking at the company from the outside, he wondered if he was entering a cult instead of a company. "I wasn't looking to join a crusade," Garner says. "But conversations with both the Gardners, as well as the Fool's board of directors (comprised of directors from blue-chip investors AOL, Maveron Equity Partners, and the Mayfield Fund), convinced him that he had nothing to worry about. "The Motley Fool was indeed truly a company. It just happened to be one with an incredibly strong culture and value set and remarkably strong ties to its customer base."

So Garner committed to coming on board enthusiastically and joined the company, appropriately enough, on April Fool's Day 2000.

In addition to clarifying the company's goals, refining its strategy, and putting in the management procedures and systems to accommodate growth and a strong bottom-line orientation, Garner says perhaps his biggest contribution has been to help the organization become more "reflective."

"I think this ties into the whole concept of Internet time," Garner says. "At a successful Internet company, I think there needs to be a learning cycle, one that is comprised of *think, act, reflect*. At the Fool, we haven't spent enough time on reflection. When we don't spend enough time reflecting, people in the company oscillate between think and act. We, like many Internet firms, were acting like a coil spring. Think was leading immediately to act and it was creating a harmonic of its own. And people can confuse that harmonic with progress.

"What has been lacking among early-stage companies in general," Garner says, "is this ability to reflect. And part of the learning for me at the Fool was not to slow things down, but to encourage the proper reflection on what we're learning by doing, before we acted again.

"And in many cases as part of that reflection—as part of that learning—you need to share what you have discovered. Everybody is so busy, that you need to make sure that the learning is shared."

This has been especially important given the volatility of the stock market and the dot.com crash, which in Garner's words, "tested the patience of even the hardiest buy-to-hold Fools." In his Halloween letter to The Motley Fool community, he offered sound advice intended to share what the company has learned as well as principles to bolster investing. "If we learned anything since last Spring, it's that even in the so-called new economy, the old rules of business still apply. As ever, substance beats out concept, cash flow trumps cash burn, and a market shattering IPO does not necessarily spell long-term shareholder value. Here at The Motley Fool, we're more focused than ever on building an enduring business and an enduring brand that serves the evolving needs of our customers—no matter what's happening out there in the stock market."

Though The Motley Fool's publicly stated mission is "to educate, amuse and enrich," in practice, the company is reinforcing a cycle that has quietly guided it for the past seven years: to learn, grow, and teach.

At The Motley Fool, learning naturally leads to teaching. It creates and continually improves a distinctive service that benefits from a virtuous cycle of intense interaction with—and feedback from—its customers.

At eBay, the next case study, the company learns from its community how to create a service that becomes more and more central to the lives of its customers. It then makes improvements and learns even more to make its product and service offerings increasingly better and more important to the people it serves.

The company is a true reflection of its customers.

CASE STUDY

eBay
The Customers Drive Everything

Even when it comes to the telling of the company's official corporate history, eBay (www.eBay.com) has learned from its customers.

The story about how the world's largest online auction site got its start is well known. Legend has it that Pierre Omidyar and his then fiancée (now wife) Pam, were talking about Pez, the candy shaped like tiny bricks that inspire cultlike devotion. The Pez dispensers are just plastic devices about six inches long by about an inch wide.

Pam is an avid Pez dispenser collector (she now has more than 400 different versions, some shaped like cartoon characters, others like animals, sports heroes, and movie stars, and just about anything else you can imagine).

According to eBay corporate lore, Pam wistfully said to Pierre:

"Wouldn't it be wonderful if there were a place where fellow Pez collectors could meet, interact, trade, and buy or sell." As an early Internet enthusiast, Pierre knew that people needed a central location to buy and sell unique items and to meet other users with similar interests. And so Pierre created a Web site to make his fiancée happy. He started eBay—"e" for electronics and "bay" for the San Francisco Bay area where they lived—in the late summer of 1995 in order to fulfill Pam's collecting need. And the rest is, as they say, history.

And so ends the tale of eBay's creation. It is a great story.

And it's almost true.

The reality is that when they were having the conversation about Pez collectors and Pierre heard the word "Pez," he thought computers. His original intention was to sell used computers in an auction-style marketplace.

He created that marketplace—details on what he decided to call it in a second—but there was a problem. Nobody came to the site to buy and sell used computers. But eventually some collectors discovered Pierre's Web site and used it to trade other things, and Omidyar was smart enough to learn from that. The site quickly evolved into being a place where Pez collectors—or anyone else— could come to buy or sell all kinds of merchandise both new or used.

Oh yes, about the name. Well, it always was eBay, but not exactly for the reasons that have now passed into legend.

Pierre wanted to call his new company Echo Bay. (Why? Simply because he liked the name.) But when it came time to register the name for Internet use, Omidyar discovered that "echobay.com" was taken. So he began using Echo Bay as the corporate name, but when it came to figuring out what to call his Web site, he shortened it—to eBay.

And that's the true story behind the company's creation. However, while the real version may be factual, the one that is now of legend is actually the one that customers prefer. The legend involves more whimsy. So that is what the company uses.

Does all this matter? On one level, no. Corporate histories, like all stories, invariably improve in the retelling. But on another level, it does. The revised corporate history is just another small example of how eBay learns from its customers. Those customers wanted the version the company tells to involve Pez dispensers and the San Francisco Bay, and so that's the way the company tells it. The story has evolved, just as the company has, because customers wanted it to, and it is customers who have made eBay one of the most popular and successful companies operating on the Internet and in the digital economy overall.

Pierre and his board of directors made one of the most significant and prescient CEO recruitments in the digital economy—actually in the entire economy—when Meg Whitman agreed to join the company in March 1998. With a diverse career from blue-chip companies such as management consultants Bain & Company, The Walt Disney Company, and Hasbro, Whitman has proved the ideal partner for Pierre and has successfully scaled the company from 138 employees when she joined to more than 1,700 today. One of her most significant management selections was bringing Brian Swette on board, first as head of marketing and then chief operating officer. Swette traded in managing a $750 million advertising budget as Pepsi-Cola's chief marketing officer for the chance to help build a new kind of brand—and business that could not have existed before the age of the Internet.

eBay has been learning from its customers since its beginning on Labor Day 1995. Those customers wanted to buy and sell more than used computers, and so Omidyar, and later CEO Meg Whitman and Chief Operating Officer Brian Swette, kept adding categories until the point where eBay has grown to become the world's largest personal online trading community and one of the most successful Internet sites by any measure you choose—usage, customer satisfaction, sales, or perhaps most important, earnings.

Today, eBay has gross merchandise sales of several billion dollars, revenues of hundreds of millions, profits of tens of millions, and a market capitalization of over $13 billion. The eBay name and concept have also become an integral part of popular culture, being frequently mentioned and demonstrated on "Oprah," "The Rosie O'Donnell Show," David Letterman's Top Ten List— even President Clinton has been pictured on television using eBay. The brand—and the trading activity that underpins it—is even being extended to network television. eBay has announced its plans to launch a television version of the site featuring items available for bidding through eBay as well as profiles of some of eBay's 22.5 million users.

Individuals—and now increasingly businesses—use eBay to buy and sell items in more than 5,500 categories, everything from Beanie Babies and sports memorabilia to consumer electronics and automobiles and fine art.

It was fashionable—and even accurate, to a large degree—to describe eBay as the nation's garage sale when it first started. (Indeed, those ubiquitous Beanie Babies made up 10% of the company's volume initially.) But those days are long gone. Any place where you can find *new* Ducati motorcycles, still-in-the-box kitchen appliances, and fresh-from-the-craftsmen Cartier watches cannot be described as a flea market or tag sale.

In total, some five million items are posted for sale at any given time, with 500,000 new items being added daily. With 79 million transactions per quarter, the company has been living up to its mission: "To help people trade practically anything on earth."

The mission statement also says something else: "The growth of the eBay community comes from meeting and exceeding the expectations of these special people."

Now, just about every company says something like that, but eBay actually uses it as key operating principle.

Brian Swette explains. "All the changes that we make on the eBay site come from our customers. Take the categories we use to sort the merchandise that is posted so that it is easy for someone to find. Figuring out what should go where may seem simple, but is not. And the customer drives our entire category structure. We actually have a team of folks that works directly with the customers to define what the categories are.

"Everything that goes up on the site, all the features, navigation, *everything* actually comes from the customer. We have a group called 'Voice of the Customer,' which is our formalized customer group. Then on top of that we draw on our most prolific sellers, who we call 'Power Sellers.' We have 1,000 key Power Sellers in the Gold Club and another 10,000 to 20,000 in the Silver. These are the people who do the most business with us and we make sure we run everything by them. They get to vote on all the things that happen on the site. We are really as customer-centric as possible."

Again, many companies say this, but eBay actually does it. To Whitman and Swette, focusing on the customers means more than just asking them what they think of proposed changes. The company seeks out their opinions directly and indirectly. First, it literally asks them for new ideas. According to Whitman, "Our 'Voice of the Customer' program, where we bring a group of real customers to our offices every month, is intended to keep reminding ourselves that eBay is not just about unique visitors, registered users, and transactions. It is about the real people behind all of those numbers." Each of the customers who are major "Power Sellers" have their own personal contact at eBay.

Second, eBay focuses on customers in an indirect way as well. Here's how that works. As the company has grown, it has attracted more and more small- and medium-sized businesses, businesses that have started using eBay as another distribution channel for their products. Noticing that, eBay now attends just about every major trade show, not only to show the flag but also to search out new marketing ideas and products that could help their sellers move merchandise. The logic behind that, Swette says, is simple.

"One of the philosophies on eBay has always been to watch the marketplace, see what is evolving and then take a small step into it. Clearly, what we found were small businesses starting to use eBay as a place to purchase products such as computers. So we decided to take our first step and try to organize that marketplace. And we were focusing on really small businesses. And, again, they're already using eBay as a platform, so our move into the marketplace isn't seen as an intrusion."

In fact, he says, it is a natural fit.

"We're an online company, and we're all about trading. And we're also about community. And community is how the company grew up. It's about shared areas of interest that made eBay successful."

"eBay hasn't been a passive utilitarian concept; it's highly evolving, as we learn from our customers. It brings a sense of gaming to it, a sense of winning, a sense of finding, and a sense of sharing common interests. So it's become part of people's lives, as they shape what it becomes."
—Brian Swette, Chief Operating Officer, eBay

All this feeds upon itself. The concept of community led naturally to a concept of what eBay calls "local trading."

"Sometimes when you want to buy or sell something on eBay you may prefer to deal locally," Swette says. "It may be an item that is either difficult or expensive to ship. You may want it quicker. You absolutely need it the next day. You may actually want to take a look at it. Or you may just have a little bit better feeling if you're buying from someone in the local community. Whatever the reason, we recognized there would be a benefit to letting customers trade within their local areas.

"So with a full team of exactly one person, we launched 53 regional sites in 1999. And ever since, it has been one of the faster growing parts of our company. It's gone from about 6% of our business to about 10%. This is, of course, while we have been doubling in growth."

YOU CAN MAKE A LOT OF MONEY
REALLY LISTENING TO YOUR CUSTOMERS

If it sounds as if eBay has reduced all this to a formula, it has. It's a formula that not only maximizes what it learns from its customers but also one that maximizes profits. In fact, eBay is one of the few Internet companies that found a business model that has been both profitable and scalable since its inception. It has no cost of goods sold. It carries no inventory, which means that it has no warehousing or shipping fees. (Cost of mailing the merchandise sold is paid for by either the buyer or the seller.)

As a result, eBay concentrates on increasing its revenues. Here's the formula eBay uses to make sure everyone at the company understands what the company is trying to do:

> **eBay Revenue** = # of Registered Users **x** % of Registered Users that Are Active **x** Listings per Active User **x** Average Selling Price per Listing **x** Commission %

The keys, as the formula demonstrates, are to acquire registered users efficiently (i.e., at low cost), and then convert them into active and loyal users who buy and sell frequently and are confident in putting ever more valuable merchandise on the site for sale. All of this will happen only if sellers find a lot of buyers for their offerings and buyers find a lot of merchandise for sale in an easy-to-use, trust-inspiring environment.

Here is how eBay makes its money.

While you can pay more to have your item appear in boldface on the eBay site, and/or be highlighted in one of the categories, there are really two primary fees to which sellers are subject (buyers never pay a fee to eBay). The first is a minimal insertion fee. The pricing structure for that looks like this:

For items priced between:	The fee is:
$0.01–$9.99	$0.30
$10.00–$24.99	$0.55
$25.00–$49.99	$1.10
$50.00–$199.99	$2.20
$200 and up	$3.30

Then there is a tiered, final value fee, or commission, which works like this:

- 5% of the first $25 received by the seller.
- 2.5% of the part of the winning bid between $25.01 up to $1,000.
- 1.25% of anything over that.

This is how that translates for a seller. Let's suppose an auction closes with a winning bid of $1,200. The commission would be assessed like this:

- 5% of the amount up to $25, or $1.25.
- 2.5% from $25.01 up to $1,000 (or 2.5% of $974.99) or $24.38.
- 1.25% of the balance over $1,000.01 (or 1.25% of $199.99) or $2.50.
  Total commission on $1,200: $28.13 or 2.34% of the selling price in this example.

As you can see from the fee structure, the key is for sellers to have a successful auction. While eBay receives minimal amounts of money from the listing fees, the real money is to be made on the commissions. That means it needs to make sure that sellers find a willing buyer.

"From the beginning, we were fanatical about creating seller success, because we knew that this was the vehicle that would make people come back," Swette says. That explains why there are discussion boards where sellers can trade ideas, but also a list of tips eBay sends out should an item not sell. (You can relist your item for free if it does not sell the first time around.)

At the same time the eBay business model is so powerful and positive, however, it has led to a challenge that the company has had to learn to address the hard way: lawsuits. With millions of transactions facilitated by the eBay trading platform and community, it is no surprise that a portion of these trades go awry. After all, trading on eBay is governed almost entirely by the honor system. This is the most powerful force governing fair play on eBay. One tool that eBay created to reinforce the cultural values of the community, which is becoming increasingly popular around the Web, is its Feedback Forum, a reciprocal system whereby buyers rate sellers and sellers rate buyers on transactions. Highly rated sellers in terms of value and quality generate increased buying attention and traffic. Sellers who get panned with low ratings next to their listings will not attract buyers. In the same vein, buyers who score highly in terms of paying promptly for their purchases and standing by their bids will score highly whereas those who do not will not be awarded winning bids.

But despite its culture of empowering and facilitating its community, there have been several situations where eBay has been forced to make tough judgments about what sellers may not offer for sale on eBay, such as firearms, human organs, and presidential votes.

Taking the trust that eBay customers put in the company a step further, the company confronted cases where people tried to hold the company accountable for fake merchandise. There have been law-

suits filed by people who say they bought autographed sports memorabilia later found to be fake. The lawsuits asserted that eBay has a
responsibility to ensure the authenticity of the merchandise sold
through its site. The company has successfully argued, however, that
eBay (merely) operates a venue for sales and cannot be held liable for
fraudulent transactions. The first two cases of this nature were dis-
missed in early 2001 effectively ratifying eBay's position. Despite
this legal success, Swette said that one of the company's most significant ongoing investments is in a sophisticated corporate counsel
and legal staff to keep the trading environment free and clear and to
minimize the risk of regulation. eBay has also learned that it pays to
make continuous effort to educate users and increase safety on the
site.

FINISHING THE WAY WE STARTED

With its organizational learning strengths, customer obsession,
powerful brand, and profitable, scalable business model, the company is bullish about the future, in spite of the challenges facing
Internet companies of late. According to Whitman, "I think this
company is truly going to be huge. We really are at the early stages
of what we are going to become. That's why eBay is a great place for
people who like the notion of pioneering."

We began by quoting from the Web site. Let's end by taking a
page from one of Meg Whitman's analyst presentations:

"At eBay you'll find the numbers [of traffic and items posted and
sold] rather astounding. But to understand the unique success of
eBay as a business, you might want to keep in mind what you won't
find here. No inventory, no warehouses, no shipping costs. And with
each day, eBay is looking less and less like just an extraordinary
Internet success story and more like something bigger—a place
where person-to-person trading of almost anything on the world
wide web can take place. Or, as *Time* magazine recently put it—eBay

is becoming an economic phenomenon second only to the stock market.

"Because when people come to eBay it doesn't matter what country we live in, whether we're rich or poor, or even what language we speak. In the end, we're all searching for something. There really is no limit to just how broad this place called eBay can be."

In the immediate aftermath of September 11, 2001, eBay demonstrated this fact in a way that pulled the power of its community together for the collective good of the New York City relief effort. It launched eBay's Auction for America, which established the goal of raising $100 million in one hundred days to support organizations including the September 11th Fund, the New York State World Trade Center Relief Fund, and the American Red Cross. The program, which is being run in conjunction with New York City and State, has attracted over 45,000 donations of merchandise and services that will be auctioned off—everything from Starbucks Latte for Life to a Tiger Woods–autographed U.S. Open flag, to a Spencer Stuart Executive Search.

eBay truly has become an exceptional company by creating a self-reinforcing, adaptive learning organization.

Success Factor #3
Obsess the Customer

Introduction

I t used to be that a company could consider itself customer friendly if it sent out surveys every so often and conducted regular focus groups. That type of customer research worked well enough during an age when product cycles were long and competition was generally predictable. (If it takes a couple of years to build the next version of your product, you only need to check in with the customer every few months.) But as technology has changed and product cycles have become dramatically compressed, it's more critical than ever to stay in tune with the customer on a real-time basis. This is what we refer to as *customer obsession*.

Customer obsession must be a key priority for the CEO if a company is truly to put consumers at the heart of all its intentions and goals. Otherwise, even the most committed efforts might go without real and lasting rewards.

Why is this principle so important? One reason: The Next Economy inverts the traditional relationship between the company and the customer. How so? Markets have become increasingly fragmented in recent years. The end result is that it costs a great deal to attract new customers and build a breakthrough brand. And if even you reach a mass market, it's incredibly costly to distribute into it.

It wasn't always like this, of course. In previous decades, for example, you could create a one-size-fits-all ad campaign featuring a typical couple endorsing the virtues of your product. The ad would run on the three major television networks and you would be assured of reaching a large majority of the people who were watching television at that time.

Today, if you ran that same ad on ABC, CBS, and NBC simultaneously, less than half of all viewers would see it. Nowadays, they tune into the dozens of other choices provided by their cable and/or satellite systems. (And besides, you could not run that same ad today—there is no such thing as a *typical* couple.)

In today's splintered television market—and television remains the best way to reach the widest audience—companies need to spend more with greater frequency to target narrower segments than ever before.

And there's another challenge: Web-based commerce and research dramatically lower a customer's cost in seeking out and switching suppliers. This gives the customer far more power—and the companies far less—than in the industrial economy. And so the relationship between customer and company gets turned on its head. Now, an organization must work harder and spend more money to find and retain every happy consumer it gets.

The power swing has been most dramatic among the packaged goods companies. Take Procter & Gamble. Up until the 1980s, P&G had enough heft to dictate to retailers which of its hundreds of brands they should take, and in what quantities. Then came the simple bar-code scanner, and overnight, supermarkets knew precisely what was selling and at what price. So the stores became more demanding. They set the terms when they negotiated with the large consumer product players like P&G.

Today, retailers are working hard to sign up "registered" customers online and treat them to special e-mail offers, newsletters, and "club" promotions. From these initiatives smart merchandisers are figuring out precisely what the consumer wants and needs, and they are pushing these requests right back to their suppliers. The cumulative effect of all these changes has been nothing less than a seismic shift in how corporations perceive their customers. The notion of customer obsession isn't just a useful strategy—for many, it's part of the corporate ethos, stitched into the very fabric of how they do business. This will become more clear as we examine the case studies up ahead.

THE CUSTOMER IS ALWAYS RIGHT NOW

One great example of customer obsession is a company we just met, eBay, the world's largest online person-to-person trading community. In the second quarter of 2000 eBay boasted over 15.8 million registered users, up from only 68,000 in the first quarter of 1998.

eBay's users don't think of the site as "the company's Web site," they consider it *their own*. In fact thousands of merchants have set up full-time businesses to peddle their wares on eBay, treating it as just another channel of distribution. And more and more small retailers are using eBay as their *only* outlet.

Before eBay even thinks about adding a new product line, such as selling cars, or changing the site to enhance the functionality, it looks to its most valued users for feedback. The company has formed Gold and Silver circles of Power Sellers with whom the company works to continue to refine the service.

"We learned from our customers that if we change eBay in ways they are not comfortable with, they'll let us know and they do so vociferously," Brian Swette, eBay's chief operating officer, says.

Is that a bad thing? Absolutely not, says Swette.

"We have learned that our customers are our strongest asset."

Beyond expanding the customer base to create larger market places for listed merchandise, a passionate community launches the "viral marketing" that helps Web-based businesses grow. In companies such as eBay and The Motley Fool, passionate customers become the de facto sales force, spreading the word about the company's virtues. Companies like eBay benefit from what's commonly referred to as the network effect—when the value of the enterprise expands exponentially as the number of users of the network increases. For eBay, sellers benefit from increased site traffic because, in general, it means higher prices on merchandise across the site. (More users means more competition, forcing the bidding to go higher and higher.) This then expands the number of sellers—after all, sellers want to list their merchandise where they think they can get the best price. That in turn draws more interested buyers and the cycle starts again—and the number of eBay network users grows even greater.

But this kind of growth will come only if you obsess on your customers and you do so relentlessly.

The next two companies you are about to meet do just that. Sun Microsystems has reinvented itself three times since its creation less than two decades ago, and each time the customer has been at the heart of its reformation. Sun's $16 billion in year 2000 revenue and $55 billion market capitalization reflects how well it has met its changing customers needs. StorageNetworks, based outside of Boston and founded only in 1998, offers its customers a way to safely store mission critical data remotely. Seemingly overnight, the company's market value shot up to $10 billion before coming down (along with the rest of the Nasdaq-listed companies) to $2 billion.

Its keen understanding of its customers allows StorageNetworks to be agile, and on target with product enhancements. Let's examine more closely how these companies "obsess their customers."

10 Ways to Obsess the Customer
1. Find out who your customer really is.
2. Create a big comments box on your Web site.
3. Show appreciation for your customers' loyalty by saying thank you.
4. Manage customer information.
5. Give customers what they want.
6. Don't neglect viral marketing.
7. Be sincere.
8. Keep things simple.
9. Personalize everything you can.
10. Be obsessive about the customer experience.

C A S E   S T U D Y
Sun Microsystems
The Sun That Rises Over the Net

The Internet is really nothing more than a vast network of computers. But not just any computers. Most of the "boxes"—computer hardware in the techie parlance—are made by Sun Microsystems. For almost any company today in the market to get online for procurement, selling, or marketing, Sun is most likely in its future.

The company's success is largely due to the efforts of Chairman and CEO Scott McNealy and his partner, President and Chief Operating Officer, Ed Zander. The duo has built a mighty empire on three pillars: Vision. Focus. Execution.

In an industry where external factors can disrupt the most carefully constructed business plan in a matter of weeks, Sun's top executives believe in stability, specifically keeping the vision of the company constant.

But that vision can extend far over the horizon.

More than 10 years ago, when Sun was primarily known—if it was known at all—for its workstations used principally by engineers, McNealy and Zander saw that the Internet, and corporate intranets, would merge. When that happened, growth in the computer industry would revolve around the World Wide Web, and not boxes. Zander and McNealy also saw that the winners in the networked era would clearly be those who could help customers adapt to this brave new (interconnected) world.

That vision—which is reflected in the company's prescient tagline: "The network is the computer"—yielded a new focus, one that would move Sun Microsystems away from workstations toward becoming the one place to turn when you wanted to get your company running on the Internet, or as the company's advertising put it, when you were ready "to dot.com" your company. In other words, Sun would evolve from a hardware company to one that was a full-blown Internet services provider—hardware, software, consulting services, whatever it would take for its customers to succeed on the Web. That is how the firm would execute.

Since the mid-1990s Zander, along with CEO Scott McNealy, has made a major push to refocus Sun on the Internet. As we saw earlier, when we were discussing the first principle, speed, a tight focus allows the organization to move faster. Their focus on the networking niche has paid off as corporate America is now scrambling to reap the benefits of electronic connections throughout the supply chain. Yes, of course, the dot.com pure play has become an endangered species. But the Sun brand is recognized well beyond the dot.com eruptions in Silicon Alley and Silicon Valley. Zander and McNealy now inhabit a niche that is large and growing larger. And they are the big player.

The company's vision—in this case Sun's decision to become a full-service Internet solutions provider—becomes the litmus test of everything the firm does going forward. The result is that Sun now provides everything it takes to get its customers on the Web, and provides tools they can use to succeed once they get there.

Here is a series of business headlines for a week chosen at random late in the year 2000.

Sun and TimeLogic Announce Alliance to Power Bioinformatics Research

Sun Microsystems and TimeLogic announced today their alliance and collaboration to provide bioinformatics researchers advanced algorithm acceleration solutions to meet their computational biology needs.

End-to-End Solution for Life Sciences

(PR Newswire)—Sun Microsystems announced today that it is strengthening its focus on the life science industry through the Sun Discovery Informatics program, an offering to enable biotechnology leaders to develop the highly synergistic and interoperable solutions needed to power the discovery pipeline. In conjunction with this program, Sun has announced the creation of the Sun Informatics Advisory Council, a consultative group whose industry leading commercial and academic members will assist in mapping out Sun's future hardware, software and service offerings for the life science industries.

WhereNet Raises $20 Million from Ford Motor, Sun Microsystems

Santa Clara, California. (Bloomberg)—WhereNet Corp., a closely held provider of software and equipment to help companies track inventory, said it raised $20 million in private financing from Ford Motor Co. and Sun Microsystems Inc.

Three different headlines, but these three different stories have one theme in common: They are all about customer obsession. In each case, Sun determined what a customer needed, and then set out to create it through:

a) a partnership, or
b) creating resources they can draw on, or
c) simply providing them funding (in exchange for taking an eq-uity stake).

The path the company follows in providing what its customers need doesn't matter. "Doing it does," says Zander.

"Once we understand the customer discontinuity, once we understand the technology discontinuity, we focus, focus, focus, on solving it and then we execute, execute, execute. We put our blinders down and just go like mad."

Being fast is not a luxury. It is a necessity since a remarkable 70% to 80% of the company's price list is replaced *every year*. So if McNealy, Zander, and their team cannot come up with new ideas and new ways to satisfy their customers, Sun is marginalized at best and out of business at worst.

IF YOU ARE GOING TO OBSESS ON THE CUSTOMER, YOU HAVE TO KEEP THINGS SIMPLE

Zander copes with his environment by continuously pounding away at making things very simple within Sun, so that tasks can be completed quickly.

"You have to keep things basic," Zander says. "You've got to have a simple vision that all your employees understand. I don't want to get into a discussion of our competitors here [Sun is a notoriously vocal and ferocious competitor of Microsoft], but I have a lot of friends who work at some competing companies and when you get turned around every six months to a year with a new strategy, a new focus, it's very hard to get all employees aligned, especially as you grow bigger.

"So, I think we work very hard at communicating to all of our 35,000-plus employees, and our customers, and our software developers which are a very important part of who we are, what we stand for and where we are going."

The vision is simple and consistent. And it has to be, Zander says.

"It takes incredible discipline to stay with what you think are the right answers. It's hard. It's complex. And it is also not easy to focus the company and execute, but we have an ability to organize in a very fluid fashion, to take some big risks. We take big bets, and so far so good."

What would be an example of one of those big bets? Well, it doesn't get any bigger than reinventing the company.

"We've truly reinvented ourselves three times now [since the company's creation in the early 1980s]. And we reinvented it from positions of strength," Zander says. "I have a formula inside of Sun that I talk about a lot and it's this: At the height of success—not at the height of failure—you break your business.

"I think that our competitors try to reinvent themselves only when they've had poor quarters or poor years. And by that point, while it is necessary, they have waited too long. Maybe if they had done it earlier, they wouldn't have had that bad quarter or that bad year.

"The real success for Apple would have been for them to reinvent themselves when they were so successful eight or ten years ago, and now they're back to where they were back then. The real issue is, can you reinvent yourself when you're growing the fastest? That is what we have tried to do at Sun. We took workstations to basically the first billion dollars in revenues. Then, seeing how our customer needs were changing, we reinvented ourselves around servers, and network computing. That got us to $10 billion. And then, determining that our customers specifically, and business in general, would migrate to the Web, we reinvented ourselves around Internet computing. Now we're on our way to $20 billion and beyond. What we have become in the last couple of years in many customers' eyes is not just a server company, but an advisor to how to re-create their businesses."

"Most technology vendors providing the products that are accelerating the Internet phenomenon today don't help customers understand how they can compete in the New Economy once they get there. They seldom focus on the pure business needs of the customer, or provide a business-oriented blueprint for their success." —Ed Zander, President and Chief Operating Officer, Sun Microsystems

The idea that companies needed to offer a place for their customers and suppliers to interact with them online has been growing over the past decade. Today most companies understand that they can gain huge benefits by working electronically with their customers and suppliers online. Sun was hearing this well before the dot.com revolution began and the hype swelled even the flimsiest business plans on the public markets. Now that the hype is long gone, Sun has still emerged as the company to turn to for companies that are serious about leveraging the Internet. That's because they've been responding to the needs of serious companies over the past decade and not just trying to turn the ship on a dime overnight. Zander explains:

"Here's what we found out on our sales calls in the last couple of years. It wasn't, 'come on in, Ed, I want to go buy a server.' It was basically: 'Come on in, Ed, I want to talk to you about "dot-coming" my company [before "dot.com" was a dirty word]. How do I do b[usiness] to b[usiness], b[usiness] to c[onsumer]? How do I get my suppliers, customers, employees webified onto the Net? What does it mean to do this stuff? How do I make the transition?' "

Those questions led to Sun's creating a consulting business which would help its clients make the transition from the "old economy" to the next one, and help them succeed once they got there.

"I think a lot of our sales guys today used to walk in and say, 'Here's a fast box,' " Zander says. "Today they walk in pretty much as an advisor and partner to these companies that are trying to remorph their businesses around the Internet. We've got as many innovative programs as we have products.

"All this came about because of listening to our customers. I remember a defining moment two years ago at an Executive Advisory Council meeting we were having. About every nine months we bring in 15 or 20 of our top customers for presentations and talks about what is happening in the business. There are no sales people or sales pitches. We spend two days just talking about issues and where the industry is heading. And I remember a day in Palm Springs a couple of years ago when we discussed strategies around the Internet, and Java applications. Toward the end I asked, 'What can Sun be doing better to help you?'

"And one of the guys raised his hand and said, 'Look, Ed, you've got great slides, and you've got great products, but what I really want is for you to come in and give us the blueprint on how to dot-com my business.'

"I remember those words, 'give us the blueprint on how to dot-com my business.' And all the other chief information officers and executives in that room said, 'Yes, products don't mean anything, tell us how to begin to blueprint what we have to do.'

"That's how our latest reinvention began. Now, at Sun before we propose an Internet solution to our customers, we start by addressing how our customers can develop and implement a Net business strategy of their own. We are very forward thinking here. We try to look at our customers, look at technology and then break the mold of the old."

In other words, if Sun can reinvent itself periodically, why not its customers?

StorageNetworks, the next company we are going to meet, received some of its pre-IPO funding from Sun. That shouldn't be surprising. The company is also a living embodiment of the principles that Zander just discussed.

CASE STUDY

StorageNetworks
"This Is All We Think About"

Peter Bell, cofounder and chief executive officer of Storage-Networks, is still in his 30s and he's already been through any number of wild gyrations navigating the twists and turns on the road to the Next Economy. Founded in the late summer of 1998, the Waltham, Massachusetts-based, company stores huge amounts of data for client companies of all sizes as well as various government agencies. From being one of the early leading players to create a new market—external data storage—to riding the IPO wave and going public within a year of its founding and garnering a $10 billion market capitalization, to keeping his team focused and the business results on track during the dot.com meltdown and Nasdaq crash, he has been forced to live by the new execution principles—or perish.

Bell said to us that he loves the company only second to his wife and family, so success is the only option. The principle he holds on to dearly—and the one that will ultimately help StorageNetworks thrive, is to be fanatical about understanding and meeting its customers' needs.

Whether you own a PC that you surf the Net on in your family room or are a *Fortune* 500 chief information officer managing hundreds of thousands of workstations and your company's mission critical information systems, the good news is that the cost of information storage continues to fall. This is good news because individuals—and companies—have come to expect that they can use and store virtually as much information as they need without thinking about details like cost, security, and capacity.

The bad news is that at some point, you can literally run out of room. All the available storage that came with your system is gone, and even if you add more, eventually you are going to reach an absolute limit on how much you can store.

If we are talking about your computer at home, it's no big deal. You either delete some files, or pull some information off your hard drive and put it on one or more disks that you keep nearby.

For corporations and governments, however, the situation is trickier. To have an easy and secure way to access its information is no less than a requirement for competitiveness. Having individual employees decide what should be stored and where can quickly become a logistical nightmare, one that is becoming more daunting by the moment. Forrester Research, for example, predicts that companies will increase their average online storage capacities by a factor of 10 over the next five years. That means, according to Forrester's projections, that unless the costs associated with storing all that information continue to fall through the efforts of StorageNetworks (and its competitors), the line-item for data storage on a company's information technology budget, will grow from the single digits, where it stands now, to 17% in 2003.

What's needed, therefore, is a different approach. Enter StorageNetworks, which handles data storage—and a lot of it. How much data does StorageNetworks store? Well, when it comes to bits and bytes, descriptions and analogies are tricky, but try this. When computer professionals talk about large groups of data, they refer to "terabytes," which roughly corresponds to as much information as you can stuff into 60,000 filing cabinets. Today, in over 40 locations worldwide, StorageNetworks is warehousing hundreds of terabytes of information (or over 6 million filing cabinets' worth) for firms that can access it instantly.

As Bell puts it "we are trying to make data storage as flexible, reliable, and easy to access as electricity or phone service. Customers want to be able to plug their computing resources into this utility where their data's always available, always accessible, and it's secure, and that is what we provide. So we're building a centrally managed network of storage resources that provides our customers with a significant value proposition because of the scale and the quality of service that we're deploying today."

Clearly, information technology managers would like to outsource the data storage function. But there is only one problem. Since data is so critical to every organization these days, potential StorageNetworks customers need to be guaranteed that offsite storage will be safe, secure, and always accessible. Otherwise, they will handle the storage themselves, regardless of the cost.

Bell is aware that StorageNetworks' clients' peace of mind is vitally important and so it literally manages its business from the customers' perspectives into the company. This is consistent with the basic tenets of sales management—but it goes further and extends beyond the sales force to the entire top management team.

"Every Monday morning at 10 A.M. we have a senior management meeting," Bell explains. "And the first thing we do is go over what we call 'red, green, yellow.' These are colors we assign to the relationships with our customers and they change all the time. During this meeting we review *every single customer* we have, and strategize about *their* business and where we are relative to their needs.

"This is how our company should be measured: If we stopped working with a client, would they truly have a challenge running their business? If that is the case, then we are doing a good job." —Peter Bell, Chief Executive Officer, StorageNetworks

"When we truly understand where they are in their businesses, we look at five things:

1. Service level, which is the base one. We want to know if the customer is satisfied;
2. Are they 'referencable' (i.e., will they be our evangelists in the market)?
3. Financially, are they paid up (after all, we are running a business);
4. Do we have a campaign under way to have them take additional services; and
5. Do we believe this customer will be with us for the long term?

We categorize into the different levels and we don't focus too heavily on the greens because green means that things are in good shape. The yellows usually mean there's some specific, defined concern, or that we haven't done a piece of the service yet. But it's the red ones where we spend a lot of time. From the reds, we really find out what is happening. We obviously fix whatever is wrong, but more importantly, we get to the root cause and then fix whatever was at the root cause that created the problem.

"We follow up on all of this every single Monday, so not only is focusing on our customers one of our core values, but we have systems in place to act on it," Bell adds.

One of those systems is "Knowledge Works," an internal Intranet where every problem—or opportunity—the company has ever encountered is logged and documented in detail. Everyone in the company has access to the database. Bell explains how it works.

"Say you are talking to the people at Deutsche Bank in London about them becoming a potential customer, and you want to find out all the banks we've done business with, what we've done and who our internal experts are. You could find all that out easily, even if you were brand-new to our company. As a result of your search, you could call up Max Riggsbee in New York who handles Merrill for us, find out what we did at Merrill, find out what mistakes we've made; you could find all the proposals, all the architecture, what worked and what didn't. We make it easy for our people to find the right internal resources who can provide all of their lessons learned. We've tried to put as much as we could in Knowledge Works so that it becomes a central information repository for all our employees."

A RECENT CUSTOMER OBSESSION

That is how StorageNetworks' customer obsession works in theory, but how about in practice?

Bell provides a specific example of something that recently happened. "Each of our customers has a service level agreement which defines and measures StorageNetworks by the levels of data availability and system up-time. But to us, those two things are just the minimum. In our culture, we believe in more than doing the minimum.

"Recently we had a customer that ran into a huge capacity constraint with no lead time. That is a serious problem because when you run out of capacity, you literally can't perform your data processing and you can't run your applications. They called us late on a Friday night, and were terrified that they just ran out of capacity. They said, 'We just didn't plan well for it. We're stuck. Help!'

"Well, under terms of our contract, we had up to 21 days to provide more capacity for that particular customer. But with our customer's business on the line, it was second nature to drop everything and get the problem solved. In what is normally a several days' process, we did it in eight hours.

"We had to scramble to find people, given that it was now the weekend, and we didn't have a pricing schedule set up for this particular requirement. But we knew we would worry about that later. Our sole focus was on getting them up and running again as quickly as possible.

"Doing this creates a couple of things. One, it creates huge strength in that one particular customer relationship. But equally important, we ended up creating a whole new set of services based on this type of requirement. Instead of finding a way to deliver a huge amount of capacity instantly as a one-off, we figured out how we could cookie cutter this. That is always one of the things we try to do. We take care of the customer in circumstances such as this that we have never encountered before, and then we ask ourselves how can we turn what we just did to solve the customer's problem into a repeatable model.

"What I particularly like about this example is that it happened without any involvement from senior management," Bell adds. "The fact that it did tells me that the values of the organization have really gotten through to the people who work here. In this particular case, solving the customer's problem started with the local sales rep and it worked its way up to the local operations person who drew on what he needed to take care of it. No one ever went for approval, and that's the way it should have been."

How does Bell instill these values into the organization?

"I give a talk to all our new employees and one of the things I always discuss is decision making. I make sure to say concentrate on looking at what's right for that customer—not just each customer, but also what's right for a *broad* set of customers. Make sure you have data to justify your decision, and then make sure the decision can be leveraged in a repeatable fashion, so that what we do is not just a one-off.

"And that is exactly what happened here. The people involved went outside the normal bounds, but that's positive because it was well thought through. They had the data, it was right for our customer, and now we're working on how do we translate what they did into what's right for a lot of customers" as part of StorageNetworks' never-ending customer obsession.

StorageNetworks' obsession about its customers revolves around these five points which comprise the company's values statement:

- Follow through on commitments
- Consistently deliver excellence
- Foster long-term relationships
- Become a trusted and respected adviser
- Deliver value every day

Success Factor #4
Reward (Appropriate) Risk-Taking and Failure

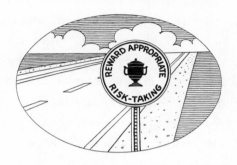

Introduction

Trial + error = experience. It's a simple formula. In the Next Economy, where many rules are being written in real time, experience is an increasingly treasured commodity. And since not every risk will pay off, that means that failure not only has to be tolerated—it should be rewarded. This is a radical departure from the experience most of us have had in the workplace.

As the deposed CEOs of Mattel, Lucent Technologies, Gillette, Xerox, Maytag, Covad, and others can painfully attest, businesses will swiftly punish failure and poor performance. But the most successful leaders today somehow find a way to balance the achievement of performance with appropriate risk-taking. In fact, they instill the value of genuinely tolerating—and even celebrating—failure, so long as learning, another one of our execution principles, is the residue of the effort.

> The feedback loops in the Next Economy are so rapid and measurable that successful companies and leaders experiment, read the results, adapt, and try again.

This execution principle has become so important that it can be seen even in the way that the world's largest companies now operate. Consider the case of America's Big Three auto companies— General Motors, Ford, and DaimlerChrysler—forming Covisint (see chapters 3 and 7), the massive Internet automotive parts marketplace. The three behemoths are betting that their enormous combined purchasing scale, which totals more than a quarter of a trillion dollars, plus another quarter of a trillion dollars when their suppliers are included, will give them enormous efficiencies and economies of scale that will allow them to drive down their component costs.

The success or failure of the effort has yet to be determined. Many in the press have turned skeptical. But what's most important is that the effort was attempted at all. It shows an entirely new level of risk-taking for the normally staid and conservative automakers. The companies galloped ahead with the concept months before— and with little assurance of—receiving regulatory approval (which was granted in late 2000). They shelved well-established plans to commercialize and grow individual exchanges, and put their respective technology partners, Commerce One and Oracle, archrivals themselves, into a new cooperative relationship. Perhaps most fundamentally, they overcame a long history of being wary of cooperative efforts on even the most benign industry issues, such as air bags, in order to put together this joint venture.

In return for their risk, the three companies have already realized substantial rewards. And they've skirted around potentially debilitating competition when it comes to electronic procurement.

So even though success, in the traditional sense, cannot yet be calculated, the participants have quickly gained a new level of understanding of how to do business in the Next Economy.

It is easy to say that a company should encourage intelligent risk-taking. After all, trying new things, and adapting based on results, has forever been the cornerstone of innovation.

In the digital economy, however, where barriers to entry are low, and the rewards for success large, new approaches need to be invented continuously by firms of all pedigrees—new economy or old—to stay ahead. And that means there are going to be setbacks. That fact, not surprisingly, may make many employees skittish. Raises, bonuses, and promotions have traditionally been based on successes, not failures. So it is up to leaders at all levels to make risk-taking a reality, not just talk.

Let me illustrate this principle with a brief example.

Spencer Stuart recently spent time on a confidential organizational diagnostic and recruiting strategy session for a major global bank, one with more than 10 million customer accounts. The firm, known for its conservative corporate culture, managed to get an Internet initiative into the market quickly enough to become an early leader in online banking.

As is often the case in building new businesses, the initiative's costs were higher, and customer growth slower, than originally projected. But rather than take the learning that the team had garnered and adapt the service to meet evolving customer needs, the bank's top management team launched an audit of the project to see if it made sense from a return on investment perspective.

You can guess the result. Internally, the project quickly became known as a loser. It had taken more money and energy than expected and the tangible payoff seemed further out on the horizon. The fact that the company had gained a leading market share was largely ignored. The project manager and the entire team had their wings clipped. The grand ideas were quickly pared down. At the same time, the bank's competitors were accelerating their moves into online banking.

We were brought in when senior managers at the bank were re-visiting their Internet strategy. By this time, they were lamenting the fact that the competition was raiding their talent and it was getting harder for them to recruit top-notch individuals.

Our advice was *not* to go out and try to find new people, but rather to reassess the messages management was sending to current employees about trying new things. The fact was that the conditions were not appropriate to bring new Internet-experienced talent into the company.

By contrast, when GeoCities was undergoing reorganization, then-CEO Tom Evans took pains to encourage idea generation without regard for the risk implied for each employee.

"The key to making the reorganization work was to eliminate the people-posturing," he says. "The way we did that was to put our-selves into a room and say, 'don't worry, at the end of this process, every single person in this room will come out a vice president of something. Okay?' So people therefore knew that they didn't have to put their own interests ahead of the organization's. We reduced the risk to each of the participants, and the company's ability to adapt to ongoing changes improved."

Making it safe to take chances is a key part of encouraging risk-taking. It comes down to communication. To change your company's thinking around success and failure it helps to change your vocabu-lary around key objectives. Rather than calling something a "failure" when it does not meet traditional goals, recognize that the original objectives may have indeed been wrong. Or perhaps the results could be better for long-term success than if the project followed the plan precisely.

In his simple but astonishing book *The Max Strategy*, Dale Dauten shows how some of the greatest innovations in business his-tory came from "failures." One of the key ingredients to their success was simply to change the vocabulary about what constituted success and failure. The core of the idea is simple: *Experiments never fail.*

Perhaps this notion—which literally helped create such famous products as Coca-Cola and Levi's blue jeans—is more apt than ever for leaders in the Next Economy.

There are lots of ways to create an organization that encourages risk-taking, as the two case studies that follow demonstrate. Yahoo! has created its culture out of a daring spirit to brave the unknown. The company hires employees based more on talent and interpersonal characteristics than on specific experience. The company wants people who want to join a crusade, who are self-reliant, and who can take pride in building something new. Taking chances is just part of the job. After all, you can't create an entirely new medium out of whole cloth without taking a couple of chances along the way.

At Wal-Mart.com, CEO Jeanne Jackson has set up a new company that builds upon the principles of an old one (Wal-Mart itself) and still gives employees plenty of room to experiment to determine what is best for its customers.

10 Ways to Reward (Appropriate) Risk-Taking and Failure

1. Create experiments, not contests.
2. Mitigate personal and organizational risk.
3. Encourage creative destruction.
4. Identify and support risk-takers.
5. Eliminate politics by establishing a true meritocracy.
6. Don't try to control everything.
7. Ask people to make a difference.
8. Encourage open and honest debate.
9. Challenge old methods.
10. Watch your competitors for signs of change and be ready to act.

Yahoo!

Do You Want to Make a Difference in the World?

It is probably one of the best-known stories about how an Internet company got its start. But this one does not involve two men working in a garage. It's about two young men working in . . . a trailer.

The tale begins eons ago in Internet time, back in 1994, when the World Wide Web was still largely in the domain of techies who had been experimenting with online discussion groups and communities for years. In the spring of that year, David Filo and Jerry Yang, Ph.D. candidates in electrical engineering at Stanford University, were looking for a way to keep track of all their favorite sites on the Internet. They decided to create a guide, which at first was not much more than a glorified list.

Before long, they found that their list, which had started as a hobby, was growing wildly and getting used regularly by friends who would help update the list.

Later that year, Filo and Yang converted the list, which they had taken to calling "Yahoo!," into a customized database that made it easy to find information online. Voilà! The world's best-known Internet guide was born.

Initially, Yahoo! was composed of two separate parts, the search engine and the list of sites the engine would search. As the Yahoo! Web site (www.yahoo.com) tells it, "Yahoo! (the list) first resided on Yang's student workstation, 'Akebono,' while the search engine was lodged on Filo's computer, 'Konishiki.' " (Filo and Yang named their machines after legendary Hawaiian sumo wrestlers.) The name Yahoo! itself is supposed to stand for "Yet Another Hierarchical Officious Oracle," but Filo and Yang insist they selected the name because they considered themselves "yahoos."

The following year, Marc Andreessen, cofounder of Netscape Communications, invited Filo and Yang to move Yahoo! over to the larger computers housed at Netscape. According to the official corporate history, the "Stanford University computer network returned to normal, and both parties benefited."

When the company reached the prodigious size of approximately seven professionals, venture capitalists from Sequoia Capital showed interest. It was then that Filo and Yang thought it was timely to bring in a seasoned technology industry veteran, Tim Koogle. T.K., as Koogle is affectionately known, had been a senior executive at Motorola and later president of a company called Intermec Corporation. He, along with Filo, Yang, President and Chief Operating Officer Jeffrey Mallett, and others led the company to its position as the bellwether of the Internet industry.

Of course, change is a constant in business. And during the turbulent period during which this book has been researched, written, and published, the juggernaut that has been Yahoo! since its founding, confronted the most serious challenge yet to its future. With the crash of dot.com advertising, which accounted for a substantial portion of its $1.1 billion year 2000 revenues, a slowing economy, and the skepticism of traditional advertisers and without new revenue streams to make up the difference quickly enough, Yahoo!'s towering market capitalization, which exceeded $100 billion in early 2000, fell to $13 billion at the end of February 2001. More significantly, the company's beloved leader, Tim Koogle, announced that he would step out of the CEO role upon finding a new executive from outside the company, which he did with the recruiting of former Warner Bros. Chairman and Co-CEO Terry Semel, who started on May 1, 2001.[1]

1. In an example of how this book interacted with "real life," I was asked, after developing a relationship with the company during the research for this case study, to lead the executive search assignment to recruit *Yahoo!*'s new CEO. The search was completed in 40 days.

Despite its significant challenges, Yahoo! retains powerful assets and advantages on which to build. It offers a comprehensive
branded network of services to more than 192 million individuals
each month worldwide. It was the first online navigational guide to
the Web and remains the leading guide in terms of traffic, advertising, household, and business user reach. Yahoo! is the most recognized and valuable Internet brand globally, and in July 2000 was
ranked the number 38 leading consumer brand worldwide according to an Interbrand study. In Internet advertising, it maintains the
market leadership position ($1.00 of every $8.00 of Internet advertising was captured by Yahoo! in 2000), a major advantage in a
time of consolidation and rationalizing marketing budgets. The
company now also provides online business and enterprise services
designed to enhance the productivity and Web presence of Yahoo!'s
clients. These services include Corporate Yahoo!, a popular customized enterprise portal solution; audio and video streaming;
store hosting and management; and Web site tools and services.
The company's global Web network has significant presence and
leadership in more than 20 countries. Now, however, with online
spending falling back to earth, the pressure is on to find new
sources of growth and diversify its revenue beyond advertising.

"PEOPLE ARE OUR MOST IMPORTANT ASSET."

This phrase has become a joke thanks to the companies that printed
it and then went on to show little if any care for their "precious assets." And that's too bad really because the point is still incredibly
valid.

In the 21st century, employees really are an organization's most
important asset—and they grow in value every day as the cost of intellectual capital increases and the supply of talented employees declines.

Since that is the case, it begs this question: What will be the keys to attracting and retaining great employees in an environment where talent will be as critical—if not more so—than financial or natural resources? Tim Koogle, who joined Yahoo! as president and CEO in 1995, says perhaps the key to answering that question may be to understand that a leader cannot do much if he has no one to lead.

"This business that I had the good fortune of running is all about intellectual property. And intellectual property is all about people."

So, what is the best way to attract and keep them?

"Employees want to work at a place where there is a stimulating environment, where their colleagues are fun and really smart, and where their actions can have an impact. That's the kind of culture we've tried to establish here from the very beginning and that is the kind of culture we always want to have here, regardless of how big we become." —Tim Koogle, former CEO, Yahoo!

"For a long time now, I have come to believe that there is one thing every single person shares. I believe that everyone, at an individual level, really wants to make a difference. Everyone on this planet wants to have a clear sense that what *they* do is meaningful. And if they're in a place where they're doing meaningful work, at whatever level they can contribute, they are going to be fulfilled.

"I think that is the key," he adds. "A lot of time in the 'attract-and-retain-people' area is spent talking about the financial incentives and rewards you put in front of employees. And frankly, I think that's important, but only up to the point where you allow individuals to be able to support themselves and actually get ahead enough to feel secure.

"Beyond that you get into an area where it is all about whether or not an individual can go work at a company where they feel they can make a difference." And by that, Koogle says, he means that the members of your organization feel they can get some satisfaction from their work, strive to be a market leader, and surround themselves with other folks who have similar goals and values.

"I think people want a combination of those three things, not one or two of them, but all three. I've always thought that those three factors are at the top of the list that employees care about. The financial stuff is sort of secondary," he adds. "It's secondary because you always have to be competitive in terms of financials. But it has to be something more than that, and that something more is the work environment."

This point has taken on increased urgency in a much more challenging market environment. For the first five years after Yahoo!'s founding, the company's stock options, which have been a core component of employees' compensation packages, rose steadily in value. The options, which save the company in payroll expense since they cost nothing to issue (except in the form of increased dilution for stockholders), are an important form of incentives, not only for Yahoo!, but for virtually all companies competing in the digital age.

This was all well and good in times of rising stock prices. But with the technology-laden Nasdaq Composite Index having fallen an astounding 63% from its high in the spring of 2000, many stock options have become worthless. (That happens when the current share price falls below the options exercise price. Employees given the option to buy stock at $20 a share obviously won't exercise that option if the stock is trading below $20.)

Options that are underwater, as the saying goes, aren't much help in retaining employees. If you've come to rely on options as a way to keep your folks happy and energized, it's probably time to find other incentives. Yahoo! knows the problem all too well. At the end of the third quarter, 2000, 14% of the options held by Yahoo!'s employees were below their issuance price; by June 2001, this number increased to more than 60%.

The lesson is clear: You've got to have more than options in your employee retention bag of tricks. For Yahoo!, the answer has been to tap into employees' deeper sense of meaning and make work more than about attaining stock-options wealth. Despite some widely reported transitions at the top of the company, such as the heads of Europe and Asia, Yahoo! still boasts among the most stable employee bases of any company in the Next Economy.

How does Yahoo! do that? By creating a work environment that allows people to experiment and thereby thrive. Koogle says that to do this, you start with the people who are going to be working at the company, not the workplace itself. You begin by hiring people who want to make a difference, and then you let them do what they do best.

Let's take the ideas one at a time.

NO "BOZOS" NEED APPLY

According to Koogle, "It's very simple what we have done at Yahoo!. We hire on the basis of two things: intelligence and proactive behavior, which involves attitude and a 'can do' spirit. In general, these two things are much more important to us than specific experience. We look for these two things because the space in which we compete is changing so fast that people need to be able to figure out for themselves what needs to be done. So we look for if they're smart and if they have the right attitude."

Koogle adds the stipulation that there are some cases where the rules don't apply, such as specialized functional roles like technology, finance, or advertising sales (for example, in mid-2000, Yahoo! recruited a Wall Street veteran, Susan Decker, formerly head of equity research at investment bank Donaldson, Lufkin & Jenrette to become the company's chief financial officer, and also recruited Gregory Coleman, formerly president of Magazine Publishing at *Reader's Digest* to become head of North American Operations with a special focus on improving relationships and effectiveness with the advertising and marketing communities). "We also have what we call the 'no Bozos rule' here at Yahoo!," Koogle says. "I actually have a little poster on my wall that says that, 'No Bozos.' We always try to hire the best; very smart people. We then try to get really clear about what the goals of the company are, and what we want to accomplish. Not because we expect these people to follow orders, but so they have a framework for when it comes time for them to execute. And then we push authority as far down in the ranks as possible, to let employees do what they can to make the company a better place.

"I'll give you a couple of examples of how that works in practice. When I joined in the summer of '95, we had about seven people. There was Jerry and David and four or five of their friends. One of those was a woman named Kelly, a very bright woman but whose original role was to help out around the office, go buy Power Bars and Cokes, stock the refrigerator, plus answer the phones for us. She was basically our office assistant.

"Kelly now runs a significant amount of our business over in sales operations. She has continued to scale, by just taking on more responsibility and learning about different parts of the company," Koogle explains. "Every time she comes across something that needs to be done, she says 'I can do that'—and she does. She now has a real significant role in driving revenue, and putting together programs for big advertisers.

When we asked Koogle what Yahoo! employees had in common, he said that it was an easy question.

"Basically, they are examples of how we hired smart people who have a really positive attitude. We do try to bring in people who are like us. We're all glass half-full kind of people. We're all saying, okay, great, we've got that, how can we actually use it to leverage into something else? We are like this, as opposed to people who say, we've got that and it's got all these limitations, therefore, we can't do this, that or the other thing. What we look for is an attitude which revolves around viewing things positively and having the spirit to go for it."

Koogle and the Yahoo! leadership team have created an environment where people try things, see how they work, adapt and respond based on the feedback they receive, and improve from there. Yahoo! employees are experimenters and are rewarded rather than reprimanded for trying out new ideas and taking risks.

BUT IT DOESN'T HURT TO BE PARANOID

Koogle is quick to point out that there is a flip side to all this at Yahoo!.

"Frankly, we are pretty paranoid," he says, "and I think that's a good thing. We constantly worry about our competition, and we actually delve into the details of what they are all about so we actually know them really well. Once we do, we then try to figure out ways of executing them. And we do this all the time, every single day.

"I think companies should be paranoid," Koogle says, borrowing the favorite word of Intel's chairman, Andy Grove. "But at the same time, they shouldn't fall victim to what I call the possum syndrome. In the Southeast of the United States, where I grew up, there are thousands upon thousands of possums, and if you've ever driven through the Southeast, you know that you see a lot of them dead on the road. A huge number of them become road kill every year, hit by cars. It's easy to understand why. They're nocturnal, and when they get out on a road at night and they see headlights coming, instead of running, they freeze. They see the headlights, they know it's danger, and yet they fail to act.

"We try to keep that in mind, when it comes to thinking about our competition. It's okay to be fearful of your competition, it's a good thing actually, but you always have to act. You have to do something, even if it turns out in retrospect to have been the wrong thing. If you fail that's fine, fail fast and get on with it."

In other words the concept of encouraging action, then reading the results and adapting to what you discover—either good or bad—

as a result of those actions is something you have to build into your culture.

Yahoo! is counting on this to take it forward successfully into its much more challenging future.

CASE STUDY

Wal-Mart.com
Building Off What You Know

Talk about risk. What happens if you are the world's largest retailer—one on track to become the world's largest corporation—and you decide to add a major new business? The short answer is that there is very little upside. If you succeed, most people will say, "Well, they have the brand name, financial muscle, management depth, purchasing scale, among other things. They were expected to do that." If you fail, then it is a disaster because you were supposed to win with all of your advantages.

Jeanne Jackson has been in exactly this challenging position as chief executive officer of Wal-Mart.com, the 6,000-store chain's official move on to the Internet. She was brought in after a distinguished career at retail giant Gap Inc., where Jackson oversaw the hugely successful Banana Republic chain of stores as well as that company's Internet efforts.

Jackson was attracted to the company because of the opportunity to build an "independent-but-linked" Internet company with Wal-Mart—a strategy intended to build on the parent company's strengths and address its challenges head on.

Consistent with best practices at the time, the Wal-Mart.com venture was launched independent of the core business in terms of its management team, the design and operation of its Web site (www.wal-mart.com compared to www.wal-martstores.com), online product selection/merchandising, customer support, marketing, and significantly, financing.

While Wal-Mart served as the angel investor for the business, the company brought in the blue-chip Silicon Valley venture capital firm Accel Partners, which acquired 20% of the venture. As a part of its investment, Accel's managing partner, Jim Breyer, accepted a seat on the four-person board of directors. Bringing in a third-party investor was intended to finance the enterprise, create a wealth-creation opportunity to attract employees, and add expertise to the company and board in terms of experience scaling a business, financial engineering, and technology. But with the elimination of the strategic and organizational threat from pre-IPO companies following the dot.com melt-down, Wal-Mart announced in July 2001 that it had bought out the minority stake in Wal-Mart.com held by Accel Partners.

As it turned out, the linkages of Wal-Mart.com to the giant retailer have proven both inexorable and powerful. So the reintegration move is accurately described by Wal-Mart executives as "more evolutionary than revolutionary." First, the online company uses the invaluable Wal-Mart name and its massive promotional power, which will drive massive traffic to the site and distinguish it from all other online retailers (e.g., placing the URL on everything from the bags at checkout to the company's trucks). Second, customers find identical merchandise pricing online as offline, ensuring that the company's massive scale results in highly competitive prices. One advantage this provides is that the site can generate additional business for Wal-Mart's stores by focusing attention on Wal-Mart shoppers who might not be aware of all the products and services the stores offer. Third, Wal-Mart's famed logistics and distribution skills and infrastructure support the online store as well, helping the company execute its operations behind the scenes. And finally, customers have the ability to return merchandise purchased online to any

Wal-Mart store, taking much of the risk and hassle out of shopping on Wal-Mart.com.

This last point is sound policy and will indeed provide a strategic competitive advantage, as is discussed below. But due to an intriguing—even counterintuitive—element that underscores Wal-Mart's online strategy, this may not be as important in reality as in perception. This is because the original premise of Wal-Mart Stores was to bring the same products and prices that urban customers enjoyed to rural America. However, as the company has become so pervasive, it is now largely only urban Americans who do not have access to Wal-Mart stores. Presently, Wal-Mart.com can provide Wal-Mart products, services, and value to customers residing principally in urban geographies where the economics of establishing hundred-thousand-square-foot stores are not viable.

With all of its advantages, the pressure is on Jackson to make Wal-Mart.com a success. The early results have been reported as solid, but there is still a long way to go to realize the company's ambitions of making Wal-Mart.com as powerful and successful on the Web as Wal-Mart is in the physical world.

The pressure on Jackson was only increased when one of her key decisions during her first year—widely perceived by the e-commerce industry as a major risk—was to shut the site down in the fall of 2000 for "remodeling."

We begin our case study with a review of this decision.

Jeanne Jackson, CEO of Wal-Mart.com, explains the decision to shut the site down this way.

"It's funny. The folks who are traditional retailers understand perfectly that when you have a really big store, it's easier to close it completely for a couple of weeks rather than try to keep it open for business while you're under construction. But the people in Silicon Valley were saying, 'It's just a site. Why don't you just put it up on the storing server and keep the thing going?'

"The reality, however, is that Wal-Mart.com *is* a store. We have over a half a million items for sale and a half a million pages of content as well as a half a million links to inventory. If you start doing the algebra, you end up with millions and millions of potential points of failure, if you are sloppy. There's almost no way you can migrate data while the store is open and not have something fail. Something's bound to go wrong. So rather than disappointing or aggravating a customer who happens to be on the site trying to order the power saw at the moment you're migrating the data on the power saw, we made the decision to just close the whole thing while we migrate all the information over. So when the customer does come to shop, they will be certain to get a reliable experience. And the economics are usually better, even though it's painful for the few weeks you're closed."

But logical though that explanation was, the decision to take the store offline until it was fixed raised eyebrows across the e-tailing landscape. For one thing, Wal-Mart was relatively late to the Internet party, launching almost five years after archrival Amazon.com. For another, it was in the eyes of many, supposed to blow away the competition once it opened its door on the Web. Remodeling was not what anyone expected.

Again, it ties back to the fact that when you work for the world's largest retailer—to give you an idea of just how large, one in two American families visits a Wal-Mart at least once a week—things are supposed to go smoothly.

Jackson understands all this. Her solution to dealing with being placed in this high-stakes position? Build off the company's core strengths, communicate constantly, and leave employees lots of room to do what is best for Wal-Mart's customers within a framework that is clear to everyone within the organization.

"Wal-Mart has a very strong history of excellence. When it comes to things that touch the customer, we have a high standard that nears perfection," Jackson says. "The company was on the third generation of the Web site, which was still not where it needed to be from a customer experience standpoint. It was hard to navigate and find exactly what you wanted, and also buying took too long.

"Senior management decided that if they got a team that was able to focus strictly on the customer, they would get a better customer experience. So they spun us out and sought venture capital as a way of funding the business. They selected Accel Partners, which has a reputation not only for being extremely smart, but because they were always a believer in the power of creating an online-offline synergy with companies that had strong brand names. I was brought in as part of that."

And while Jackson did not scrap everything that came before her, when she decided that wholesale remodeling of Wal-Mart.com was called for, she did return to basics.

"Our three rules when we went to design the site were reliability, ease of use, and security," she explains. "I knew when we did it over, we were going to get slammed by some of the Silicon Valley techno-wizards for the fact that it's a very simple site. There are no bells and whistles. It is easy to navigate and find what you're looking for. The search capability is terrific. Our product images are huge. And customers should be able to have a very good purchasing experience for the product. It's incredibly reliable, and hopefully customers will really find it easy."

In making over the Web site in this way, Jackson was keeping with the Wal-Mart tradition of doing whatever it could to enhance its relationship with its customers.

Of course, it could be confusing for some customers to confront a company that has both retail stores and an online presence. And if both units are set up as separate enterprises conflicts and confusion are inevitable. Role models have been few and far between in terms of a retailer successfully setting up an independent-but-linked Internet company. Barnes & Noble was the first major retailer to create a separate Internet company based on the same brand, Barnesandnoble. com. But BN.com, as it is now known, has only recently become linked to the parent company[2] with regard to pricing, marketing, and returns. And Staples.com, the online unit of the giant office products retailer, was also brought back into the core business of Staples as a part of its Staples Direct Division. In fact, as of late 2001, the trend was for carve-out e-commerce companies to be brought back into the fold of the parent company, such as in the case of Wal-Mart.com. But the fact is that the jury is still out in terms of the winning independent-but-linked e-tailing strategy.

Jackson, a retail veteran, has always been cognizant of the potential trouble spots, and she's gone to great lengths to mitigate the problems. "We truly act as if there are not two companies in everything that's important. And that everything includes customers, flow of product, and relationship with suppliers. As far as we're concerned in our day-to-day workings, we're one company, because we're one brand. And we would start confusing customers and suppliers if we started acting like two separate companies with two separate agendas in the way we transact with them. That would be suicide.

"This goes back to the core values in the Wal-Mart brand, which are very clear and well understood by every Wal-Mart associate. It's all about the customer, first, second, third, fourth, and fifth through tenth. It's also about being reliable and offering great value. Every associate takes those three things into account with every decision they make.

"When you have these things as your operating principles, integrating two separate companies becomes fairly easy, because you

---

2. Barnesandnoble.com is a joint venture between Barnes & Noble and Bertelsmann—it also has public shareholders.

know what you need to do, and that is do what's right for the customer," Jackson adds. "And so if the best customer experience has a
transaction occurring via the Internet, then we do that. If the best customer experience has a transaction occurring in the store, then we
do that."

Take product returns, for example. While Jackson said that it was
only natural for the company to accept returns from Wal-Mart.com
at any Wal-Mart store, for many retailers processing returns from
their sites is a notoriously difficult policy to implement. This is the
case for several reasons, some seemingly simple, some obviously difficult. For some retailers, basic operations such as financial and
inventory management systems cannot adequately account for products returned through a different channel. In other cases, the barriers are no more complicated than how P&L statements are put
together, such as when products not sold by that particular store or
region are penalized for taking back product. In still other cases, retailers lack the logistics systems and skills to handle product returns
coming into multiple points in the field rather than to a central
clearinghouse.

But at Wal-Mart.com, this was never going to be an issue. As
Jackson explains, "When we decided how we would handle the
situation of a customer buying something on our site, and not liking it—for whatever reason, there was not even a real discussion.
It was, 'Okay, what's good for the customer?' And the answer,
of course, is to give the customer the option of returning the item
at their nearest Wal-Mart store. Once we came to that conclusion—
and it didn't take long—we said, 'Let's now figure out the best system
to make that work.' " Wal-Mart would never do anything for internal
accounting that disadvantages the customer. It has long been guided
by the principle of making the decision that is right for the customer,
and taking care of the accounting later. In addition, the company's
famed distribution and logistics team was able to develop the optimal
approach for how to deal with the product returns most efficiently.

"I think if you start out with a vision for the business that is rooted in a company's long-standing values and areas of expertise," Jackson says, "conflicting decisions that come up become much easier to deal with. Our vision for this business has always been about quality products, great values, and making customers happy. The logical extension of that is that we wanted our online store to be easy and reliable. If you have a very strong touchstone, it makes decisions a lot easier when stuff comes flying at you. You can either say, 'No, that's not our strategy. We're not going to do that.' Or, 'This is critical to our strategy. Let's make sure we have someone capable running it.' "

Again, once employees know the ground rules, they are free to improvise. Two quick examples underscore the point.

Wal-Mart.com has adopted Wal-Mart's "sundown rule," which was created by Sam Walton, the company's legendary patriarch. The sundown rule says that when something comes your way, make sure it's resolved for the person who sent it to you by sundown. "We have gotten into this rhythm where we do our e-mails at night," Jackson states. "And we e-mail each other at the end of the day saying either 'I took care of that, and here's what I did,' or if we haven't resolved something, 'Here's what I am going to do about it tomorrow.' We tell them what we're doing about it and when we will get it resolved. This way you don't have these dangling things out there like, gee, I wonder if so-and-so's ever going to get back to me about that request I made for something. We get back to each other quickly even if we don't have the answer. It's just another way of reinforcing personal accountability."

As is the way Jackson has adopted Wal-Mart's "10-foot rule," the company's policy that if the customer gets within 10 feet of you, you acknowledge them, you ask if you can help them, and if they ask you to help them, you help them. For example, if the customer asks, "Where are the coffeemakers?" the associate walks them over to that department, instead of saying, "It is two aisles down on your right."

"As a result of the 10-foot rule, one of the places where we are investing in headcount and payroll is our customer help center. The reason is that this is the area that customers will have the only human contact with us. So we want to be able to build a capability where we can handle whatever issues come up quickly. For example, let's say a customer calls in and has a problem with a TV set that came from an outside vendor. Rather than refer them to that outside vendor's call center, which is standard practice in the retailing industry, because it allows you to off-load the problem, our help center associates say, 'I will call Sony, I will solve the problem and I will get back to you.' Or they will stay on the phone and set up a conference call. In our minds, we own that customer. And we own the customer by making sure that he or she is happy."

COMMUNICATE, COMMUNICATE, COMMUNICATE

In a new organization that is separate but inexorably linked to a parent organization, how do you get these kinds of messages across? How do you let people know that they are more likely to get into trouble for *not* trying something new within the construct of values and culture, than for taking an intelligent risk that doesn't work out?

You start by communicating continuously within the organization. At Wal-Mart.com, that communication takes many forms, Jackson says.

"We are really focused right now on our communication with Wal-Mart stores, making sure we're aligned, making sure our goals are lined up, making sure we're not disappointing each other. And then obviously, the second line of communication, once we feel we've got everybody lined up, is going to be to tell customers what we want to offer to them, and make sure we are doing a good job of delivering on that. Only then would it be appropriate to communicate externally," Jackson adds.

"But the biggest audience for us are the people running the Wal-

Mart stores to make sure we get their help in making decisions. Remember, Wal-Mart has 2,900 stores and almost a million associates. Our next priority is our customers. These two places are where we concentrated our communications efforts early on."

"If you think you can only make decisions with the CEO, you're wrong. And if you think you can only make decisions by doing presentations to store managers, you're wrong. Everybody in the chain who has some kind of decision-making authority needs to understand the business at the level that it involves them. If they don't, your decision gets blocked at whatever level you're not communicating with." —Jeanne Jackson, CEO, Wal-Mart.com

But how does that communication really work at Wal-Mart.com and what can others learn from it? Jackson describes the communication path she followed.

"We start at the top, with our board of directors. At the moment, our board consists of Lee Scott, CEO of Wal-Mart Stores, Rob Walton, chairman of Wal-Mart Stores, Jim Breyer of Accel Partners, and myself. For the time being, there are only four of us, and we make sure we have clear agreement about our goals and objectives.

"At the next level down, which is the operating leadership at Wal-Mart, we have what we call the Idea Board, six members of the Wal-Mart executive team who we count on to help refine our strategies and tactics. We meet with them once every other month and we take global ideas and talk about how we make them work. For example, we've discussed things like creating an online bridal registry, which would really help the stores, and delve into how we would build and implement that. We're able to come up with ideas and create business plans around them because we have their buy in.

"At another level, we have a district manager advisory group that helps us figure out the impact of any of these big ideas on the stores.

As a result of their comments, we can either give the stores the tools to make it work, and incorporate things that will make it better, or we can avoid doing something that will be a major heartburn. So the DM advisory board is very important. We meet with them quarterly.

"Then there is the company-wide communication. Wal-Mart's internal communication process is phenomenal. There are two meetings a year where they bring all store managers to a convention center, along with the assistant managers and the associate managers. They talk about how to run their stores better and what kinds of products are most important. And I have an opportunity at those meetings to address every store manager with, number one, what is going on at Wal-Mart.com and, number two, their role in making this a success.

"Then, moving on to the most important level, which is the sales associates, Wal-Mart has, again, the most incredible communication network which is threefold. There is a computer-based learning program that is just unbelievable. There is software, for example, that teaches the associates how to take a return and why it's important that they do it right. Going through the module is required for the associates who work the help desk.

"We also have the Wal-Mart television and radio networks, two different networks that are broadcast into the stores informing associates of what's important at Wal-Mart. And we get scheduled in as one of the programs so we can explain what's going on at Wal-Mart.com. Wal-Mart radio also plays constantly and is a consistent means to carry our messages.

"I think if you miss any layer you are potentially leaving a hole where what you are trying to do can get blocked. By communicating this way, we are including every employee in the process, including them in the idea phase, and including them in the strategy."

Of course, by communicating this way and building on the parent company's values, culture, and resources, it establishes parameters in which employees are expected to operate, and lets employees have input, to suggest new ideas and take new risks.

And by establishing Wal-Mart.com as an independent-but-linked company, they will have the greatest chance for success and employees will have real potential to be rewarded for winning ideas.

CHAPTER 7

Success Factor #5
Absorb Uncertainty

Introduction

E even before the events of September 11, the world seemed to be spinning out of control. With the economy sputtering, the markets stalling, volatility accelerating, technological change accelerating, and fears of layoffs insidiously working their way into organizational consciousness, employees everywhere were unsettled. With fears both rational and irrational exacerbating these difficult conditions, most professionals found themselves somewhere between anxious and immobilized.

The need for business leadership to address this challenge is the order of the day. And frankly, it has never been more important. Business leaders need to step into the void and bring stability to disconcerted workers.

In today's world, there is a fundamental conflict at play and it falls on the leader to resolve it. On the one hand, it is self-evident that political, economic, and business conditions are continually changing. When this is coupled with market gyrations and technological dislocations, companies know that they need to be flexible and adaptive in order to thrive. One the other hand, poeple have always had a fundamental need for stability and order. Current conditions have only increased the basic human need for constancy and "answers." You just have to look at the spike in religious observance to bear this out.

Absorb uncertainty. This phrase was first coined by Akamai Technologies Chairman and CEO George Conrades, who has made an art out of rolling with the punches.

It's not easy to keep a corporation focused while reacting to external forces that are beyond anyone's control. How does it work?

One formula is: 1) to be visible, 2) to make decisions—even if you need to make adjustments as you go, and 3) to communicate aggressively and effectively.

Since you aren't about to bring the world to a halt or hobble the frenzied pace of technological change, you need a plan to deal with the uncertainty that results. A good leader, CEO, or project manager learns to live with uncertainty and help the organization do the same. They don't ignore grim realities, they simply become acclimated to living with doubt—the way Californians live with the threat of earthquakes. Yes, everyone knows that the "big one" could hit and wipe out a major city at any moment. But it doesn't keep people from living their lives and doing their jobs.

The first step of absorbing uncertainty is to be visible—to fill the void. In difficult times, people watch the leader for signals to gauge how to react—just as, in turbulence, airline passengers crane their necks to look at the flight attendants for comforting reassurance that "things are normal." If a business leader is absent, then employees' imaginations can take over, creating angst. Among the governmental and business leaders that won kudos for how they dealt with the crises, it was the likes of Mayor Rudolph Guiliani and

American Airlines CEO Donald Carty, who seemed to be everywhere.

But more than just being in the right place at the right time, leaders have to say the right things. Communicating aggressively and in a way that is tailored to the audience is therefore the second step in absorbing uncertainty. According to Ronald A. Heifetz, Director of the Leadership Education Project at Harvard University's John F. Kennedy School of Government and author of *Leadership Without Easy Answers*, "The role of the leader is first to help people face reality, and then to mobilize them to make change." A leader cannot communicate effectively by sugarcoating the news or telling people what they want to hear. They need to clearly articulate the reality of a situation, but translate it into words and concepts that people can relate to in their own way. It bears mentioning the sometimes obvious point that people filter whatever information they get through the lens of "What does it mean for me?" Consciously explaining the implications of what is going on will help people deal much better with the uncertainty of the situation. For example, people need answers to such questions as "Will this help or hurt our competitive position? How do we plan to react? What are the next steps? How does this fit into our broader plan of action?"

The third component of absorbing uncertainty is to use smart management processes to drive decision making, even when all the answers are not apparent. In difficult and uncertain times, relentless focus and an emphasis on execution will win out.

As Conrades explains it, "We all operate in an environment where there is an enormous amount of uncertainty. You, and the people you work with, cannot be sure what is going to happen tomorrow, never mind next year. The danger is that the uncertainty can lead to paralysis. You can spend so much time trying to nail down all the possibilities and all the risks that you never get around to taking action. And if you become indecisive, then you're dead. Because in today's world, if you don't take action, someone else will."

Conrades sees himself as the one who takes all that doubt and transforms it into a course of action. "I'm the guy in the organization who says, 'Okay, we've talked enough (for example) about whether we are going to do streaming media. Hell, yes, we are going to do streaming media. Let's do it and see what happens.' By me taking on the risk, I free the organization to act."

He adds, "Absorbing uncertainty does not mean getting rid of uncertainty. The uncertainty is always there and it always will be there. We understand that and in fact it is built into the way we manage the business."

In Akamai's management meetings, which are frequently characterized by aggressive and direct debate, Conrades is the one who plays referee, the person who steps back from the fray, synthesizes the respective arguments, and makes sure things are moving forward rather than in a circle. This is the role of top managers and executives. At some point any team needs to be released of all their self-doubt and let loose to move forward with a course of action. The fact is that most people crave leadership that can *protect* them from change—not instigate it. But since continuous change and adaptability is an important requirement of success in the Next Economy, a leader must accurately gauge the level of tumult and pressure that the organization can withstand before its tensile strength reaches the point of insidious fracture. As a leader of a company or a project team, you need to be the single point of accountability and a courageous decision maker. But just because you are the ultimate decision maker does not mean that you should not solicit and incorporate advice, information, and feedback from others. In fact, during the heat of battle, a great leader will gather all the relevant input from the right sources—having been well organized ahead of time—and then make a decision, communicating what has been decided and why. But again, the key is to decide and decide quickly.

We will see how all this plays out in the General Motors case study that follows. Rick Wagoner and Mark Hogan, CEO and e-commerce chief respectively at GM, have helped the world's largest automotive company unleash the power of its scale, brands, and resources by charting a course and communicating continuously how it is using the Internet to transform the company.

10 Ways to Absorb Uncertainty

1. Take action!
2. Don't unleash change all at once—start slowly and build momentum.
3. Be visible.
4. Remind those who work for you that anxiety is natural in an uncertain situation.
5. Let people know how your plans affect them.
6. Keep everyone involved, but make sure that participation in change initiatives is a matter of choice.
7. Be open, rather than secretive.
8. Fix problems ahead of you, not behind you.
9. Don't let little things take over.
10. When you change your mind, admit it.

CASE STUDY

General Motors/e-GM
Driving the World's Largest Auto Company Forward

Girth. That's probably the best way to describe a century-old, $180 billion company with 400,000 employees. And that's General Motors. To make the most of new technology, the company's leaders must grapple with a myriad of puzzling and daunting challenges posed by the sheer girth of the organization. GM is burdened with long-standing traditions, legacy infrastructure, union minefields, channel conflicts—to name just a few of the considerations. Heap on an economic slowdown in 2001 and heavy reliance on an antiquated business model. Recognizing the need for substantial change, the company's top executives have made dramatic moves: They recently nixed the venerated Oldsmobile division because of weak sales and lopped off 6,000 employees in the U.S. and U.K. The

103-year-old brand had become the weakest performer among GM's full-line divisions, which include Chevrolet, Buick, Pontiac, Cadillac, and GMC Trucks.

As the company sheds its former self, it is lurching forward into a new high-tech reality. GM has now launched major e-business initiatives across every part of its diverse organization and is spending hundreds of millions of dollars to fuel the effort. One major initiative is to use the Internet to electronically link together product planning, manufacturing, distribution, and the retail experience into a seamless environment that will reduce the order to delivery time. Another critical piece of GM's e-business transformation is Covisint, the central electronic marketplace for the flow of billions of dollars' worth of material from automotive suppliers to the major car manufacturers. As detailed in the Commerce One case study in chapter 3, Covisint is the joint venture of GM, Ford, DaimlerChrysler, Nissan, and Renault.

How about GM's business-to-consumer Internet efforts? In August 1999 GM launched e-GM, a separate business unit, to unify the company's consumer-oriented e-business efforts. The goal was to help dissolve redundancies and create a single technological architecture for the world's third largest corporation.

The giant step forward for GM never would have been attainable had it not been for strong and persistent leadership. When Rick Wagoner, a 23-year GM veteran, became chief executive in June 2000, he made it clear that e-business was one of the most important priorities at GM. Wagoner said at the time that "the Internet is a massive force that is going to change our business and all businesses." Like other e-businesses profiled in this book, GM's efforts are clearly being championed from the top. Wagoner is pressing the pedal to the metal because e-business may be GM's last, best hope to regain the luster it once had as not only the world's largest auto company, but the most successful as well. "We don't just want to be big," Wagoner says, "we want to be big and fast. And e-business is the way to be fast. It's the key way to change and rally people. Being out in front energizes people."

These are positive words of encouragement—even fighting words. But for a company as large and bureaucratic as GM, the best initiatives can be smothered into submission by inertia and institutional complacency. So when it became clear to Wagoner and GM's Strategy Board in 1998 that the Internet was going to radically change the landscape, especially in the business-to-consumer marketplace, the company moved quickly to establish a more focused, company-wide e-business effort. By creating e-GM as the company's Internet business division, GM was determined to eliminate the technological redundancies that had sprung up across the company's e-business initiatives and catalyze the effort to sell vehicles online. e-GM was given the same autonomy as any vehicle business unit, which allowed the new group to gain immediate cachet inside the company.

To spearhead the e-GM effort, Wagoner chose Mark Hogan, a 27-year GM veteran, who had most recently served as general manager for the GM North America Car Group. Hogan had no Internet or technology background and by all accounts was a "car guy" who had built his career in operations, business planning, and International. In addition to his deep GM and automotive experience, there was another advantage to his background. He was not burdened by formal technology constraints and was known as a free thinker who moved quickly and got things done. Under Hogan, e-GM oversees the company's consumer-focused e-businesses, including the BuyPower Web site and the OnStar division.

DRIVING CUSTOMERS TO THE WEB

By the late 1990s it became clear to GM that consumers had already embraced the Web as a critical part of their automotive shopping experience. The Internet was not just for books, CDs, and videos anymore. Web pure plays like AutoBytel and Cars.com were—at the time—forcing the established companies to pay serious attention to the Internet's potential. Online shopping was already having a serious impact on the sale of vehicles, and GM knew that it had to become a player. Consumers demanded it. If they couldn't buy direct, as the dot.com start-ups had promised (but failed to deliver), they could certainly change the buying experience dramatically by shopping online prior to a dealer visit. So in 1997 GM launched GM BuyPower, a Web site for consumers to help them choose and find vehicles. GM estimated that a traditional visit to a car dealership took two to three hours before a sale or lease could be finalized. A customer using BuyPower could handle so much of the shopping experience online that the dealer visit could be reduced to minutes. In this way, the dealers remained part of the process and felt less threatened.

Today, BuyPower is the engine for all GM's online vehicle information around the world. On the site, consumers can shop for vehicles, choose models, colors, and options as well as locate local dealers who have the desired vehicles for sale. Though U.S. franchise laws prohibit direct sales of cars from companies like GM to consumers, BuyPower was set up to work through dealers—rather than around them—addressing one of the most knotty challenges in e-business: channel conflict. Getting the dealer network behind the GM e-business effort has been a major challenge, but the company is making real progress. This will become increasingly important because it is through BuyPower that GM's ambitious Order to Delivery initiative will be launched over the next few years.

Today, BuyPower is up and running in 15 countries and the goal is to be in 48 countries by the end of 2001. In Brazil, for example, GM has already seen the power of selling online. Since GM Brazil launched its new Chevrolet Celta in September 2000, for example, 55% of the 15,500 cars sold in the first three months were through the local GM Web site in Brazil. But GM's dealers in Brazil got into the act as well. They set up Internet kiosks in the dealerships and did 95% of the sales through them.

Hogan says that plans are under way to adopt the Brazilian model for selling Saturn vehicles in the United States sometime in 2001 or 2002. Similar plans have already been set in motion in Vauxhall, England. Hogan says that despite the fact that the United States has regulatory issues and franchise laws, the customer is becoming more and more comfortable with the Internet. And this demand is what will lead to actual buying online at some point in the near future.

Another part of the BuyPower strategy has been to set up a series of alliances to increase traffic to the Web site. As chapter 8 details, every company will need to be skilled at striking partnerships and doing deals to win in the Next Economy, but GM had not previously been known for its joint-venturing mastery. However, it has struck some deals that are impressive as much for how well they segment the customer base as for their broad-based reach.

"We created a pretty sweeping alliance with AOL, which we announced in 2000, and we also have a deal with Net Zero, the largest free Internet portal," Hogan says, referring to the baseline relationships for driving mass traffic to BuyPower. "But it is our deals with Kelley Blue Book and Edmunds that are more surprising." These two are "infomediaries," automotive information services, which supply used car pricing and data to highly interested customers. "We know from experience that if an individual visits Kelley Blue Book or Edmunds, they are 80% likely to buy a vehicle within the next two weeks," Hogan points out. "So we negotiated exclusive links with them to secure these customers on the verge of their purchase."

A second part of e-GM's alliance strategy involves reaching out to a series of targeted communities. "We know we're under represented with African-American, with Hispanic, and with Asian customers," Hogan says. "So we've set out to create alliances with companies like Black Voices, the largest African American community on line. We've also established an alliance with Univision, which is the largest Hispanic community. And we're also working on another one with Asian Americans.

"This is a good way for us to interact with those customers, understand their needs, and be more proactive in dealing with these communities. Another of our target customer segments is mothers, who happen to make a majority of auto purchasing decisions. As a result, we have struck a major alliance with a company called ClubMom, which boasts over one million moms as members. We also have an exclusive arrangement with College Club, which reaches three million college kids, another priority segment for us longer term. In addition, we have completed an alliance with I Can, which is one of the best sites for disabled individuals. We know disabled people have a big need for transportation and services that GM can provide. And we're trying to be proactive in understanding what those specific needs are. So we're pretty proud of that one, too.

"Through all of our alliances," Hogan adds, "we've increased our web traffic by 2000%; we are now up to two million unique visits per month [a level comparable to major stand-alone Internet content companies]. If we look out three years, we think we'll have 20% to 30% of GM's total sales coming through this channel either directly or indirectly." This translates to between approximately $40 billion and $55 billion in automotive purchases executed through or directed by the GM site, illustrating just how significantly the Internet has come of age.

THE ORGANIZATIONAL IMPACT

e-GM has had a major impact inside the company as well. The business unit is housed in GM's old headquarters building in Detroit and has the feel of an early-stage technology company with orange floors and open areas for team-based collaboration, as opposed to the traditional formal office environment. In a company as conservative as GM, it may appear to be the anomaly on the fringe. After

all, e-GM employs only 150 people—or 0.037% of the company total. But Hogan receives thousands of requests from employees to
join the unit. The staff is a diverse group of technology veterans
from such companies as IBM, AT&T, and EDS, as well as MBAs
and graduate technical people who would not have typically worked
for GM. "We are able to pick the cream of the crop because of our
Internet efforts," Hogan says. "People see the world's largest Internet
startup as something to sink your teeth into."

When recruiting, Hogan purposely looked both inside and outside GM for unconventional thinkers. "Very consciously, we brought
in people who, from a Myers-Briggs' standpoint, were extroverts and
not traditional automotive industry-type thinkers," he says. "We
knew we had to be a catalyst for change in the company. In fact, it
all starts with me. I've never been billed as a traditional thinker."

Hogan says that he has learned some key lessons from the e-GM
experience already. Though he knew little about e-business when he
took the position, he understood the potential. He believes having a
combination of executives who are Web-savvy yet understand traditional business is the crucial combination. Another key lesson, which
needs to be consistently applied by change leaders in large corporations, is how to communicate effectively.

THE POWER OF COMMUNICATION

With a strategy as ambitious and a change program as significant as
GM's, how do you keep employees from being overwhelmed or dis-
enchanted?

"Communicate, communicate, communicate," Hogan says in response. "I spend a lot of my time communicating internally with top
executives, and with various business units throughout the world.
And I have also charged my troops with doing it too. All of our
e-GM people have great communications skills. It's another of the
most important qualities that we seek in our hiring. In general, it is

even more important than technical capabilities, much of which can be learned on the job." In fact the e-GM team has been described as a core of missionaries, rather than mercenaries, whose job is to spread the word. It is true that e-business efforts need evangelists, people who are zealous, resilient, and great at communicating.

"We began with a massive communication to everyone in the company," says Hogan. "Then we posted it on our internal website. And we followed it up with regular communications through newsletters, speeches, and videos. The second thing we did was to have Rick Wagoner speak about the initiative again and again. We didn't really understand the power of the single message coming from the CEO mouth until we were five months into this. I'd say that during the third and fourth quarters of 1999, we struggled with having a lack of a clear and loud message about the importance of e-commerce. But that changed once Rick took up the mantle. Rick has made e-commerce one of his top four objectives, and he consistently makes that known to our people. We are not dictating what the answer is, because none of us knows *exactly* what that is yet, but he is giving them the framework so that they can think about—and get comfortable with the possibilities."

Hogan has also learned not to underestimate the need to communicate up and across rather than just down into the organization. "I spent the majority of my time in the first year communicating down and out, and I took for granted too much at the top levels of the company," Hogan says. "We needed to do a smarter job of communication with the top ten or fifteen people in the company."

LAUNCH AND LEARN

Another key lesson is a concept that Hogan and Wagoner dubbed "launch-and-learn." Traditional companies like GM tend to be so focused on gathering and analyzing endless reams of data that it becomes uncomfortable to launch a new initiative without some type of certainty about how it will turn out. This is especially true when turning out new automobiles. They have to be perfect because people's lives depend on their safety. "You just can't afford to do that in e-business," Hogan says. "Time will whack you in this kind of space. You have to be fast and aggressive and you might not have the 100% perfect answer."

For Hogan and e-GM, the challenge is nothing less than to change the perception of the entire corporation. Obviously, e-GM will be measured by its success in driving car sales but it will also be judged by its ability to cross-market the whole realm of GM products and services. "We really want the customer to think about GM not just as a vehicle manufacturer, but as a provider of other services as well," Hogan says, referring to GM's financial services, Direct TV and OnStar services.

ONSTAR

If anything at GM convinced Wagoner that "launch-and-learn" is the right e-business philosophy, it is the OnStar system that is becoming a standard feature on almost all GM cars and trucks. OnStar became a separate GM division in 1996. The system began as a way to offer consumers a better safety and information service directly inside their vehicles. Building on the initial OnStar technology, which provided pioneering global positioning systems and cellular communications devices as a part of the car, GM has, over the years, ramped up the OnStar effort to include a set of new technologies that tie the vehicle directly to the Internet.

OnStar began as a three-way partnership between GM, Hughes Electronics, and EDS. Hughes brought cellular technology, EDS provided its call center expertise, and GM built the cars and trucks. The three companies struggled to work together, however, and in 1996 GM bought out the business and set up OnStar in Troy, Michigan, as a wholly owned subsidiary.

When e-GM was created, Wagoner decided that OnStar was such a critical piece of the e-business strategy that he placed it under Hogan's leadership. For Hogan, OnStar represented a breakthrough, a way to deliver the Internet directly to the vehicle.

"OnStar represents a constant day-to-day, moment-to-moment potential interaction with our customers," Hogan says. "And we're eventually going to enable all of our customers to have OnStar-like services in their vehicle. We've got 120 million customers on the road right now. So we're very excited about the potential of giving a broad service to our customers so that they can reach out and get whatever they need at any moment of the day or night."

Hogan provides some evolution of the OnStar service offering. "OnStar started out as a safety and security platform. If your vehicle was in an accident and your airbag deployed, we would call you on your car phone and ask if you were okay. If there were no answer, we'd immediately send an emergency vehicle to take care of you. We've saved lives with that service," Hogan points out proudly.

"We've since been able to expand OnStar to offer navigation information, because of its global positioning capabilities. With our satellites, we know where you are within a meter or two and we can tell you where to go if you're lost. We can also give you concierge service if you want to, for example, find a good restaurant in a city you're not familiar with. We'll even make the reservation for you. The same thing goes for other services that you may need. For example, if you have to send flowers because you forgot about your anniversary, we can do that for you, too. You are now able to place all your cellular phone calls without taking your hands off the steering wheel through voice recognition. And to that we are adding what we call our Virtual Advisor."

With Virtual Advisor, a driver pushes the OnStar button on the dashboard and then speaks via a tiny speaker housed under the rearview mirror to a voice-activated call center. The driver is connected to the Web and uses a security code number to gain access.

Once online, the driver can access unlimited information from the Internet including stock quotes, weather, sports information, and e-mail, all personally tailored to that driver and delivered by an automated voice response system.

"You know, there is pending legislation in 23 states to prohibit hand-held cellular telephone usage in the car," Hogan stresses. "We're already seeing those prohibitions in place in Japan and Germany. And so we think that a hands free solution is definitely the way to go and we intend to be in the lead with that."

With OnStar, GM is transforming the relationship with the customer, using technology as a sort of Trojan Horse. "We are no longer interested in simply selling people new cars and trucks," Wagoner says. "We want to sell them the most effective automotive experience. Retail financing is part of the automotive experience, having good parts is part of the automotive experience, and today, so is OnStar." Since OnStar allows the driver, who spends more and more time behind the wheel, to spend that time more efficiently and safely, customer satisfaction and loyalty should increase. "Every day we are figuring out more things we can do through the OnStar entree into the vehicle," Wagoner says. "We don't know how far that can go."

TYING IT ALL TOGETHER

GM understands that beneath all the technology and its ancillary services, there lies a fundamental relationship that cannot be ignored: the customer and the car. At the end of the day, the product is the thing that translates into profits and will halt the company's slide in market share. In order to compete effectively, GM must build innovative vehicles that inspire customers to buy.

Hogan points out that well over half of GM's products in the pipeline have no predecessor in the current lineup. "We're really heading out on a track of innovation that will change the way people view our vehicles," Hogan says. He mentions upcoming models like the Buick Rendevous, the Cadillac Evoq, the Chevrolet Avalanche, and Corvette Z06 as examples of vehicles that are not "your father's GM cars."

But in a company that sells nearly nine million vehicles each year, the hot cars sometimes go unnoticed among the more familiar ones that are required to accommodate such a vast customer base. More important to GM's long-term success will be the ability of the company to leverage technology to transform itself so that it can move faster, design and introduce greater numbers of vehicles that appeal to all of its customer segments, and increase the operational efficiency in all of its activities. For a company the size of GM, the e-business transformation turns out to be more a matter of culture than technical competence.

Through e-GM, Wagoner and Hogan have attempted to institute a "go fast" culture to challenge the company and change its mindset. Wagoner realizes that the process is not necessarily natural inside a mega-corporation like GM. But the biggest problem is not people seeking to avoid the Internet or thwart the e-business priority. Rather, it is for the huge company to genuinely adopt an attitude that asks, "How can we learn, how can we stay ahead, how can we engage our customers, our partners, the dealers, and our suppliers?"

One might not have normally thought that these are the kinds of questions that GM is committed to answering, but e-GM is helping the company do just that.

CHAPTER 8

Success Factor #6
Master Deal-Making and Partnering

Introduction

I t's been said that deal-making is an art. It takes finesse and personality, and some of us are just better at it than others. True, we can't all be Donald Trump (nor would we want to be), but deal-making is critical to the success of any business. The fact is, most businesses can't grow fast enough on their own. It's as simple as that. Product cycles are so compressed and technology smarts so dispersed, that few would deign to go it entirely alone nowadays. Partnering has become one of the single-most critical initiatives that separates the truly dynamic and successful companies from the second-tier players.

But partnering isn't just a symptom of a hypercompetitive, hyperfast economy; it's actually tightly tied to all of the other execution principles in this book. And that's part of the larger message of *Zoom*. The principles cannot be seen as lone initiatives. Rather, they are tied together. Isolate any one principle and you may or may not gain the footing you are looking for in the market. But find the ways in which they can be interconnected in your organizations, and you may find lasting value and true innovation. Here are just a few examples to see how partnering is interconnected to some of our other principles.

- **Partnerships Enable Speed:** If you learn that you are short on a specific skill set, such as engineers or salespeople, or lack a product or service required to satisfy your customers, such as data storage (as we saw in the case of StorageNetworks), a solid partnership may fill the gap. To stay speedy, it's not always necessary or even advisable to build every piece of the empire.
- **Partnerships Demand Obsessing on the Customer:** To distribute to a fragmented or tough-to-reach market (as we saw in the case of e-GM), the right strategic partner comes in handy. Obsessively understanding your customers, their interests, and where they spend their time online or offline, and then creating alliances to meet them on their proverbial home turf, has become a hallmark of successful marketing strategies in the digital age.
- **Partnerships Can Create Uncertainty:** With deals comes uncertainty and constant jostling. A leader must keep to the core mission even as the company gets pulled in new directions through strong partners. And all the while, employees must be kept assured that new partners aren't threats, but opportunities.

Deals come in all shapes and sizes. There's the outright acquisition. But there are also marketing agreements, strategic partnerships, and exclusive licensing agreements. Deal-making has long been a mainstay of businesses in Asia and Europe, according to Booz Allen & Hamilton consultants John Harbison and Peter Pekar, Jr., coauthors of *Smart Alliances: A Practical Guide to Repeatable Success.* But American CEOs have only recently begun to put an emphasis on growth through alliances. The partnership craze has been spurred on by globalization, technology, and intense competition.

One of America's most storied CEOs, Jack Welch, has long recognized the critical value of partnering: "If you think you can go it alone in today's global economy, you are highly mistaken," says Welch. It's a sentiment that's now echoed throughout executive suites everywhere. Gary Reiner, Chief Information Officer of General Electric, elaborates. "We do about a deal a day and look at another eight," says Reiner. "We have some extraordinarily talented people here at corporate that came to GE because deal making is a full time–plus job. They came out of the top firms in their disciplines, including the investment banks, accounting firms, and management consultancies." The company has spun out many creative deals through its GE Capital unit, which has grown to account for nearly 41% of the company's total earnings. But many deals come from corporate. In fact, the company's largest acquisition effort—the ill-fated $45 billion purchase of Honeywell, which was scuttled by regulators in Europe—came straight from the top.

It's time to take a closer look at precisely what makes a solid and successful e-business deal. Tim Koogle is a good person to ask. The former CEO of Yahoo! and his team have orchestrated hundreds of partnership deals to help Yahoo! become a dominant player online. "I think some aspects of a successful deal vary from one deal to another, but it comes down to fundamental values," said Koogle. That sounds a bit trite. But Koogle has a profound belief that win/win deals are the best kind. He recognizes that when the scales are unfairly tipped in one company's direction, a deal typically won't have lasting value. "At the end of the day, I think great business is done between people."

Throughout the dot.com boom, Yahoo! was true to this principle and the company earned a reputation for being a savvy and tough but fair deal-maker. This isn't the case for all consumer-oriented Net companies: "Unlike some Internet players that target consumer audiences, Yahoo! works with partners at an appropriate level based on their stage of readiness," says Conrades, CEO of Akamai. "They really helped us along when we were just starting out and they didn't try to crush us back then. After we were more developed and clearly on our way towards standing alone, they expected more from us, but they continued to be fair and to keep the process open and productive."

The ability to make deals swiftly—and integrate partners into a smooth flow of business—has become a sustainable competitive advantage. Cisco has proved this principle time and time again and is the star of the first case study in this chapter. The company attacks new markets and gains greater efficiency by being a hawk always on the search for its quarry. The company has acquired new technologies and new companies at an astounding pace. And in spite of cyclical market activities, the company continues to build through strategic partnerships and acquisitions. After Cisco we then shine the spotlight on BEA Systems, our second case study. The company, whose market capitalization is $6 billion (down from a high of $35 billion), has grown quickly out of nimble partnerships and solid technology.

10 Ways to Master Deal-Making and Partnering

1. Figure out what you do well, and what you don't.
2. Don't let deals linger.
3. Partnerships and deals need attention.
4. Make sure both parties benefit.
5. Don't let prior relationships supersede your business objectives.
6. Find the best partner you can, but don't hold out for perfection.
7. Share a common vision with your partner.
8. Produce short-term wins.
9. Create a long-term strategy even for short-term deals.
10. Consider proximity and distance as a part of the deal calculation.

Cisco Systems
The Master Deal-Makers

One of the ways I reviewed our research for the development of this book was to ask the leaders, employees, and analysts we interviewed whom they look to as role models. Which companies do they admire and study when they want to learn how to execute better?

When it came to principles such as speed, learning, customer obsession, rewarding people for taking risk, and absorbing uncertainty, we got numerous nominees.

But when we asked about who *they* studied when it came to deal-making, the answer was invariably the same:

"Cisco."

"Cisco."

"Cisco."

Given Cisco's track record of successfully acquiring companies, that should not have been surprising. In fact, it really was expected. The company has acquired more than 60 companies in the past decade and an amazing 22 in the year 2000 alone. In total, acquired companies contribute more than 40% of the company's $25 billion in annual revenue (projected to exceed $30 billion in 2001). Acquisitions have been a key part of Chairman and CEO John Chambers's growth strategy ever since the former IBM and Wang executive assumed the top job at the California-based company in 1994. From the beginning, acquisitions have helped Cisco adopt potentially disruptive technologies, enter new markets like optics rapidly, and bring in scarce technical talent. And they are key to the company's future success.

When Chambers joined Cisco in 1991 as an executive vice president, he had a simple, but ambitious goal. Borrowing a page from the Jack Welch play book at GE, Chambers set off—and succeeded in making Cisco the No. 1 or No. 2 player (with at least 25% market share) in every major computer networking segment. His ultimate objective is to provide one-stop computer networking and Internet infrastructure shopping for his customers. Acquisition was really the only way to pull off his mission quickly in a volatile and rapidly changing market. The thinking boiled down to this: If Cisco couldn't build what it needed to satisfy its customers, it would buy it. Indeed, that guiding logic would be at the heart of the company's strategy going forward.

Chambers gets—and deserves—the lion's share of the credit for effectively managing Cisco's climb to the top of the networking-equipment world: revenue growth in 44 consecutive quarters and annual growth in excess of 40% every year (with the exception of 1998's 31% growth) from the time it went public on February 16, 1990. While 2001 revenue growth is projected to slow to a rate of 20% and earnings are projected to decline by 24%, analysts still see Cisco recording annual earnings growth of 25% over the next 3 to 5 years. The company, which retains the P/E ratio of a growth stock—39x—remains firmly in the leadership position of the networking in-dustry, which will continue to be at the heart of the technology and communications revolution sweeping the world.

In addition to Chambers, there is another key executive who has also been at the heart of Cisco's success, Michelangelo "Mike" Volpi. As head of Cisco's acquisition team, Volpi has built one of the most powerful business development operations in America today.

As the company's Web site (www.Cisco.com) puts it:

Our strategic alliances are designed to help deliver a customer-centric, total solutions approach to solving problems, exploiting business opportunity, and creating sustainable competitive ad-vantage for our customers. This shared commitment to deliver solutions and services encompassing products, applications, systems integration, and best practices, will help make our customers successful as globally networked organizations in the new economy.

The relentless focus on partnering and acquisition has turned Cisco into a machine that can assimilate new technologies and companies into its system with little friction. As *Fortune* magazine said in a piece on the company in late 2000:

> No company typifies the new world of M & A better than Cisco Systems. To find a business that has handled acquisitions as well, you might have to go back to the A T & T of the early part of the 20th century, when Theodore Vail, its legendary CEO, bought hundreds of tiny phone companies and assembled the first nationwide network, giving birth to Ma Bell.

John Chambers was happy to share with me his thought process and management system for making successful acquisitions. Let's start by first reviewing a cross-section of Cisco's recent acquisitions, which demonstrates the company's strategy of filling in its product line and worldwide employee base with strategic transactions.

Recent Cisco Acquisitions

Acquired	ArrowPoint Communications, Inc.
Key Technology	*Optimizes delivery of Web content for Internet service providers and others.* A content-switching platform provides a new level of intelligence for creating content-aware features and offering users a faster, richer Web experience.
Number of Employees	337

Location   Acton, Massachusetts, U.S.A.

Acquired   **Atlantech Technologies**

Key   *Offers advanced network management for service*
Technology   *providers.* Standards-based, network management
                software configures and monitors multivendor
                telecommunication networks, including those that
                integrate data, voice, and video.
Number of
Employees   120

Location   Glasgow, Scotland

Acquired   **Growth Networks, Inc.**

Key   *Enables terabit performance for service provider*
Technology   *networks.* Internet switching fabrics, a new category
                of networking silicon, support service provider net-
                works that scale to tens of terabits per second.
Number of
Employees   53

Location   Mountain View, California, U.S.A.

Acquired   **InfoGear Technology Corporation**

Key   *Supports information appliances.* Software platforms
Technology   that remotely manage information appliances for
                Internet access help service providers and others
                deliver integrated services and customized content.
Number of
Emloyees   74

Location   Redwood City, California, U.S.A.

Acquired	JetCell, Inc.
Key Technology	*Extends Cisco's AVVID architecture into the wireless domain.* In-building wireless telephony that integrates IP telephony with traditional PBXs enables cellular phones to access corporate voice services and roam between corporate and public cellular networks.
Number of Employees	46
Location	Menlo Park, California, U.S.A.

Acquired	Pentacom, Ltd.
Key Technology	*Supports end-to-end IP-based networks for advanced services.* Spatial Reuse Protocol transports IP-over-fiber networks, allowing service providers' IP-based metropolitan networks to offer the same benefits as SONET-based networks with double the bandwidth efficiency.
Number of Employees	48
Location	Herzliya, Israel

Acquired	SightPath, Inc.
Key Technology	*Offers intelligent content delivery for enterprise customers.* Content networks deliver data-intensive applications such as real-time video, online training, and high-reliability hosting.
Number of Employees	76
Location	Waltham, Massachusetts, U.S.A.

Acquired	Subsidiary of Seagull Semiconductor, Ltd.
Key Technology	*Supports next-generation terabit routers.* High-speed silicon expertise accelerates the development of terabit routers.
Number of Employees	17
Location	Herzliya, Israel

This list represents a diverse group of companies spread around the globe. And yet, in each instance, Cisco uses the same criteria, techniques, and system to pull an acquired property into its orbit. Cisco managers begin with understanding whatever technology is needed and then prioritize the company's efforts: "Can we build the necessary technology? If not, can we create the right partnership? If not, then we become determined to acquire it, since there is not enough time to build the product from scratch." If the answer comes back "we need to buy," the company team sets off to determine who has exactly what it needs. For that, Cisco turns to Mike Volpi and his high-powered business development team, which has mapped the diverse sectors of the technology and communications landscape and maintains an up-to-date assessment of which companies are the best in each sector.

In addition, Cisco's top management consults with its customers, who form a huge network of contact points in the technology industry. For example, US West (now called Media One) was a driving force behind Cisco's decision a couple of years ago to buy NetSpeed, a maker of equipment that turns regular phone lines into high-speed digital subscriber line (DSL) data conduits. The head of US West had told Chambers that his company wanted to buy DSL services from NetSpeed, but that US West was reluctant to rely on a small supplier for what could be a significant product. Chambers saw the opportunity as clear as day and jumped all over NetSpeed.

THE FORMULA

Having bought so many companies, Chambers has a handle on what it takes for an acquisition to be successful. He has crystallized his thinking into a 5-step formula that begins by having the company look only at companies that have a chance of being acquired. The company does not do hostile deals and it does not stray from its core business.

"Everybody in the industry would say we are very good at the implementation of acquisitions," Chambers told me. "But what really makes them successful is the selection process up front."

In the best of all possible worlds, Cisco is looking for a company that has a great proprietary technological product that is six months to a year away from being introduced in the marketplace. The analogy company officials use in describing companies of this type is that they are acquiring "a seed," and it is Cisco's job to supply the dirt and water to help it grow. Acquiring a mature company, these Cisco executives argue, is like trying to transplant a tree. It can be done. But it is much harder and by definition there won't be as much growth. That is why they try to acquire smaller firms. But that objective is flexible whereas the general approach to acquisitions is more rigid.

Here are the five steps Cisco follows in every deal to increase its chances of making the acquisition succeed:

1. **There needs to be a common vision between the two companies.** As Cisco's engineers examine the technology, and its strategy and finance officers review the company's business plans and financial statements, Cisco's senior management team also assesses the vision and quality of the potential acquiree's top management team. In addition, since Cisco often acquires a company as much for its talent as for its technology or customer relationships—indeed more than a third of Cisco's senior management came to the company through an acquisition—it needs to focus

on the more qualitative issues of vision, culture, and goals early in the process. To the extent that they share a common vision for how the company's products or services will meet Cisco's customers needs and how the company and its people will fit into Cisco's world, surprises later on will be minimized. In general, life is much easier when management teams on both sides of the bargaining table see the world the same way.

2. **Almost immediately, you have to produce short-term wins, or people at both companies will lose interest.** For example, in the NetSpeed deal mentioned above, NetSpeed started getting more business from US West than it could have possibly expected or handled before the acquisition went through.

3. **There has to be long-term strategic potential behind the deal.** Not only must the acquisition fill an immediate hole in the Cisco product line and/or add critical talent, the company to be acquired needs to make sense in the context of Cisco's long-term strategy. A key part of this is making sure that the company is bought at just the right time. It must be far enough along in its own development to have a viable product, yet still be young enough to be flexible and open to becoming part of something larger than itself. Cisco has learned that it is extremely difficult to meld the cultures of two fully mature companies. Says Chambers: "I don't believe that mergers of equals work."

4. **There needs to be good chemistry between the people at both companies.** Company officials are quick to cite—off the record—the names of companies Cisco did not acquire because the chemistry was lacking. In one aborted deal, different parts of the company to be acquired negotiated separately with Cisco, trying to maximize their position at the expense of their colleagues. Given the factions, Cisco ultimately decided to pass. But when there is good chemistry, deals are more straightforward to do. As the CEO of one firm Cisco acquired puts it: "If the people fit, everything else works out." That former CEO is now a Cisco senior manager.

5. **Geographic proximity and stock options help a lot.** Chambers does not want the talent he acquires to leave. As a result, he personally spends a lot of time understanding what will keep top talent from fleeing after the ink dries. Earlier in the 1990s, this meant that the majority of Cisco's acquisitions were companies based in the heart of Silicon Valley. (Indeed, eight of the company's first nine acquisitions were located in Santa Clara County, home of Silicon Valley.) But now that Cisco is a global company, it can also comfortably go after acquisitions in Europe, Asia, and the Middle East, leveraging its office network—although the company still tries to acquire companies that are located in proximity to Cisco offices (i.e., building a campus concept). And in an industry where talent is key, attracting the best is an art, one that Cisco has mastered. One of the keys? Valuable stock options. Given the long-term strength of the company's stock—up, on a split adjusted basis, from 8.1 cents a share in February 1990 to $20.50 in June 1991, a 69% compound annual growth rate—many Cisco employees, including hundreds who have joined as a result of acquisition, have become multimillionaires. Of course, with Cisco's stock down about 75% from its high of $79 a share in March 2000, this part of the formula becomes a growing challenge.

These five points are the key to Cisco's acquisition strategy. "It's as simple as that," Chambers says. "If all five factors are not present, it's a warning light. We might go ahead with the deal, we might not. But if two or more of them are missing, we definitely walk away because we know there is going to be trouble. This formula has proven itself over time. When we stay with it, we are successful most of the time. When we violate it, we normally get into trouble."

Not only does the formula increase the odds of success, knowing exactly what to look for increases the speed at which the deal can take place. (After all, the need to move quickly is a key driver behind making acquisitions.)

Knowing the rules and the formula for success allows Cisco to move at lightning speed. Chambers and company shoot for a time frame measured in weeks rather than months (typical of most corporations) between when the senior managers propose a deal and the basics of the acquisitions are complete. That speed is possible in part because Cisco does not rely on outside experts such as investment bankers. All deals are handled in-house by Volpi's business development team, which has become a magnet for the best financial engineering and deal talent, rivaling the top M&A firms.

INTEGRATION

Acquiring a company is one thing. Making sure it fits and the people stick around is another. Cisco has a dedicated staff of 20 people who do nothing but make sure the companies that it buys mesh following an acquisition. A group from Cisco stays at the company from the start of the acquisition to the day the deal closes. And even before the deal closes, every employee in the company being acquired receives a customized packet of information that includes descriptions of Cisco's management structure and employee benefits, a contact sheet, and an explanation of the strategic importance of the newly acquired company.

The day the acquisition is announced, members of Cisco's human resources and business development teams travel to the acquired company's headquarters and meet in small groups with people from the acquired company. They answer questions and explain what it means to be a Cisco employee. Simultaneously, those new employees are put on the Cisco payroll, and automatically enrolled in the stock option plan. Nothing is left to chance.

How well does this work?

> When Cisco absorbs a company, it makes a no-layoffs pledge; its turnover rate for employees acquired through mergers is a scant 2.1%, vs. an industry average of more than 20%.

Cisco's mastery of deal-making is going to be put to the test in the months ahead. Acquisitions are the key to penetrating Cisco's priority growth segments: optical networking, Internet telephony, wireless networking, and the management of traffic over networks. But with the stock far down off its high, acquisitions are becoming more expensive at the same time that employee morale is under pressure. Last year, Cisco doubled its employee ranks, for example, meaning that at least half the workforce have options that are under water. So Chambers and Volpi are refining their approach to acquisitions, partnerships, and investments. Instead of acquiring large companies, such as optical-equipment maker Cerent Corp., acquired for $7 billion in September 1999, they are setting their sights on smaller companies that can provide product growth without lots of employees that would raise ongoing costs. Cisco is also moving more aggressively into the role of venture capitalist. While Cisco has traditionally watched early-stage companies closely and acquired them when their technology was proven, today, as venture funding is more difficult to secure, Cisco is providing funding. In January 2001, for example, Cisco committed $1.05 billion for a venture fund to be managed by Softbank Corp. in Asia.

The stakes for getting it right are huge. Chambers insists that Cisco can continue to grow between 30% and 50% annually over the next five years. At that rate, it would be a $110 billion company by 2005, nearly as large as General Electric (which took more than 100 years to reach that scale). With the economy in tough shape and ferocious competition showing no signs of abatement, such growth may seem fanciful. But consider this. No matter what happens to the economy, almost all projections call for the Internet to keep growing—traffic is still doubling every 100 days or so. With this underlying growth and Cisco's mastery of deal-making, odds are that the company will continue to thrive—even zoom ahead.

BEA Systems isn't nearly as well known as Cisco, but that might not last for long. The company is rapidly growing a formidable empire in the new and emerging application server space. One key to growth has been its Cisco-like focus on partnering and acquisition. Here's how they've pulled it all together.

CASE   STUDY

BEA Systems
Partnering with Your Customers

On most Web sites, partners get a passing mention, if there is a mention at all.

There may be a tab on the home page labeled "partners" and if you click on it you probably will find listed several companies that are more often than not really customers of the company whose Web site you are visiting.

It is not that way on the BEA Systems Web site (www.bea.com). For openers, the list of partners fills several screens. Everyone from Amazon.com to Unisys is listed, within six separate categories of partner—independent software vendor, systems integrator, consultant, application service provider, value added reseller, or strategic platform vendor.

And when BEA talks about a partnership, it means a true partnership.

"At BEA, we have modified our business model to make the substantial expansion of our global partner initiatives a top priority," says William (Bill) T. Coleman III, founder, chairman, and chief executive officer.

"We are committed to investing aggressively in strategic partnerships so that our customers can do business with us easily through familiar and established relationships, and so we can keep up with the tremendous market demand for our e-business software platform," says Coleman, a graduate of the U.S. Air Force

Academy, who began his career as chief of satellite operations in the office of the Secretary of the Air Force.

Coleman made big news in January 2001 by pledging $250 million to the University of Colorado, the largest gift ever made to a public institution. He explained to me why BEA, whose products help handle more than half of all e-commerce transactions on the World Wide Web, has taken this route and why mastering partnerships is one of the keys to its success.

To understand why partnering is so important to BEA—the company takes its name from the first initial of its founders' first names, Bill Coleman, Ed Scott, and Alfred Chuang—it is important to understand what it does. The San Jose, California-based, company has become the leading supplier of "application servers," which is essentially a package of software that offers quick, easy ways to perform common computing tasks associated with building and running a Web site.

The company's Web site gives a particularly good description using one of its clients as an example. All of the transactions you learn about in this description are handled by a BEA product.

When a consumer surfs on Amazon.com, the Web page is automatically personalized, tailored to the customer's particular interests based on his or her previous interactions with the site. That's the first transaction information is retrieved from a database to generate a personalized Web page.

Each time the customer searches for a title or author, or adds an item to his or her shopping cart, more transactions are executed. And when the customer hits "buy" after entering credit card and other information, yet another transaction happens.

Each interaction spawns a complex transaction chain. Is the ordered book or CD in stock? In which warehouse? How will it be shipped? Would the customer like to consider related titles? Is the credit card still valid? Each time the customer initiates a purchase, the site in turn transacts with the product supplier, financial databases, shipping concerns, and so on—a set of multiple business-to-business and business-to-consumer interactions that adds up to a dynamic, personalized service.

It's complex—and exhausting to think about—and BEA products are involved with the process from beginning to end.

Given how integral BEA becomes to a company such as an Amazon, teaming up with these companies as partners just makes sound strategic sense. Working so closely with clients allows BEA, which was founded in January 1995, to get constant feedback that allows it to create new products faster.

"This business is not driven by technology, it's really driven by our customers' customers. And whatever BEA's customers' customers want, BEA will provide," Coleman says. "Taking that approach will help both of us grow market share. And savvy deal-making was required as well, to grow rapidly enough to compete effectively against the giants of the software world, Microsoft, Oracle, and IBM.

"We know that as the demand for e-commerce solutions continues to increase, it will be vital to establish and maintain strategic partnerships worldwide. Only through collaboration can we meet the escalating demand with the levels of speed, quality and completeness that customers require. Hence, BEA's number one priority is our new partner initiative. We are investing in a worldwide program to make it easy and profitable to partner with BEA, and we are changing our business operations to establish, support and extend strategic partner relationships."

The approach is clearly working. BEA now has 89 offices in 30 countries, serving over 8,000 customers including the majority of the *Fortune* Global 100. With a growth rate of nearly 80%, the company generated $820 million in revenues and $17 million in net income in 2000.

OWN THE TRANSACTION

Product is everything for BEA—and that's above all partnerships for BEA. "That's the key," says Coleman. "If you own the transaction, you can make money," Coleman says. "Whoever owns the transaction owns the business and that's what we concentrate on. We've branded ourselves around being an e-commerce transactions company. The company that serves the customers that serves the e-generation.

"That was our starting point. The three of us began by saying let's figure out a plan on how to address this market. And one of the first things we concluded, and remember this was the mid-1990s, was that the technology would enable companies before the end of the decade to address large applications on the Internet. Transactions wouldn't require a mainframe. As we said when I was at Sun Microsystems, *'The Network Is the Computer.'* "

And that conclusion led almost immediately to another. BEA would have to get large in a hurry.

"Our analysis was that if we weren't at a $500 million to a $1 billion run rate by the end of the decade, by the time transactions on the Internet really took off, we would not have the scale to effectively address the market," explains Coleman. "So that's when we came up with the realization that we had to build our business on acquisitions. We wanted to form our company with products we could sell immediately. To the extent the market required, we would continuously transform the company, working on culture and business processes."

So the teaming up—at first through acquisitions—started from day one. The first acquisition was of a transaction-processing product called Tuxedo and its leading distributors, which were being underutilized by the large software company Novell. BEA acquired Tuxedo for what seemed like an enormous price in 1996, $92

million. That deal was followed in 1997 with the acquisition of a
Common Object Request Broker Architecture (CORBA) and an
object request broker (ORB) from Digital Equipment. From there,
the company was well on its way.

In September 1998 BEA acquired software company WebLogic,
which had created a rudimentary application server, for $160 mil-
lion. Since then, BEA has added to its product line by acquiring several companies, including the Theory Center in November 1999.
With all of these companies and their technologies, BEA was then
able to build on to these products and introduced a number of integrated new services, including what is now called BEA WebLogic
E-Business Platform (which Coleman describes as "the industry's
first object-based transaction monitor which enables large-scale enterprises to quickly build applications using reusable components").
On the partnering front, BEA signed a major licensing agreement
with Sun Microsystems, enabling the development of server-side
Java, and the company bought NCR Corp.'s Top End transaction
processing product family as well as a chunk of NCR's Top End development and services teams.

All of this put BEA in place to start doing deals where it could
become intertwined with its customers. One such customer is
Accenture (formerly known as Andersen Consulting), and its product EasyTax, which works with revenue agencies (such as the IRS)
around the world, and serves as a case in point. Developed in conjunction with the consulting giant, EasyTax is built on BEA's
WebLogic Server and gives revenue agencies—which not surprisingly are institutions not universally adored—a chance to improve
their relations with their customers, i.e., taxpayers, by making all interactions more efficient.

With advanced computing, communications, and content technologies, EasyTax allows customers to conduct most of their business with revenue agencies over the Internet in a simple, safe, and
secure environment. EasyTax allows them to file their returns electronically and make payments over the Internet. It also provides an

extensive customer information system which allows taxpayers the ability to answer many of their questions on their own.

"Our expanding partnership with Accenture is important to BEA's success for several reasons," says Matt Green, senior vice president of worldwide operations for BEA. "Both firms win by providing BEA technology to the established Accenture client base. Together, we meet the demand for access to best-of-breed e-business infrastructure software solutions, and BEA gains important new business relationships."

EXTENDING THE PARTNERSHIP APPROACH

Partnering with your customers will work best if you partner with your employees as well. That is, it will succeed only if the leader gives employees the chance to operate on their own, subject to the guidelines the company establishes. Coleman has a strong point of view about the best way to allow that to happen.

"I believe that if you're trying to build fast, you have to build top down. You have to bring in the people that have done it before, managers who know how to hire the people that can get the work done. That's what the three of us did from the beginning. We eventually recruited a CFO and the four of us ran the company until about the end of 1999.

"My philosophy was that I wanted everyone who was on the startup management team to have been an executive in a large company, an executive in a startup and have been through at least one failure. And all four of us had done this. I wanted that because I don't think you learn how to survive a failure until you've been through one. And all companies, no matter how successful, have to weather downturns."

"I lived through the first personal computer software wave in my VisiCorp days. And the psychology in the market then, and the psychology on the part of the people working in the Internet today, is largely the

same, 'We're inventing the world, nobody's ever done this before, all the rules have changed; long term is three months.'

"That's all baloney. The reality is that every generation has done this. Everybody wanted something new. People get passionate and work really hard, they think they're doing something different than anyone else. But because everyone is doing this, everyone starts in the same place. And the ones that win, I believe, are the ones that build to last with a long-term vision, where they don't sacrifice anything for the short-term." —Bill Coleman, Cofounder and CEO, BEA Systems

"The way you build this kind of a company fast is you build it based on personal empowerment, which in turn is based on open information," says Coleman. "As CEO, you don't make all that many decisions. You start with a vision and you put a culture in place that empowers people to make decisions and move them as close as possible to the point where they can be executed.

"The only real challenge for BEA from day one has been management bandwidth," Coleman says. "Everything else follows when you have the right culture and you're hiring the right people who know how to grow people, and you empower them. They are really the ones who build the organization and get everything done. If you follow this route, you end up with an approach that's more strategic than tactical. But this way, there are no constraints on your growth. It all depends on your people."

And those people, of course, are often the ones building the company and pursuing the next round of deals and strategic partnerships.

"We do not define ourselves by our products. We define ourselves by the market that we're going after," Coleman says. "We're going after the application infrastructure market. That's it. We're not going to be an application, we're not going to be an operating system, and we're not a network. We are going to enable the transactions. And so the question we ask is: What does it take for our customers to be able to quickly build applications that are reliable and can be adapted on the fly to meet the changing world of the Internet? Now, that application infrastructure is changing on a monthly basis; it's an expanding universe so we have to be close to our customers, we have to partner with them, so we can change and evolve almost as quickly as the market does. That way we both succeed."

A lot of people are counting on Coleman being right. According to industry reports, BEA garnered 32% of the market for application servers and software last year, double that of IBM, its nearest rival. But as the company matures, it will have to generate more service revenues to offset market saturation, while at the same time continuing to develop winning products that businesses simply cannot do without. BEA is therefore in a position that is simultaneously powerful and anxiety-producing. It is the lead company in a rapidly growing field, smack in the middle of e-business. But its competitors are among the most powerful in the world, with hundreds of billions of dollars of cash and market value to compete for the most attractive deals, people, and products.

But that does not faze Bill Coleman. He believes that by 2005, BEA will be one of the top three software companies in the world in terms of revenue, market capitalization, and earnings.

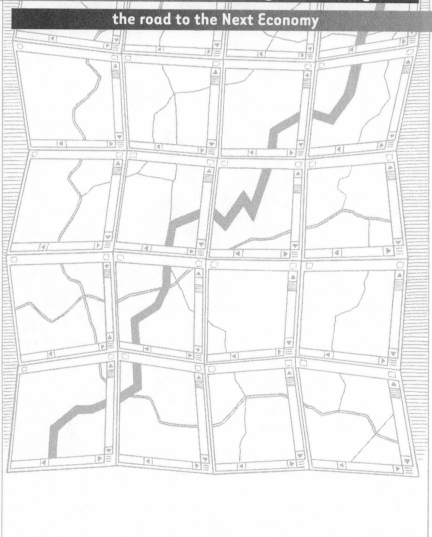

PART III

Hitting the Open Road

Weaving the 6 success factors together to navigate
the road to the Next Economy

CHAPTER 9

Execute!

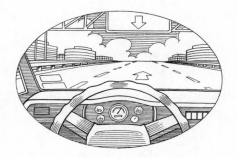

A year ago, some pundits claimed that business cycles no longer existed. Thanks to automation, the American corporation was supposedly capable of keeping in perfect synch with demand. We were being told that jeans or sneakers or refrigerators would never again collect dust in warehouses because they wouldn't be manufactured unless the consumer wanted them. It's an economist's dream. Unfortunately, as recent history shows, we haven't come close to reaching that point.

While it is true that companies have gotten better at managing inventory, we still, for the time being, live with the inevitable boom-and-bust cycles that have characterized capitalism since its beginnings. The stock market has its inhale-exhale pattern, too. The real questions are: Who can successfully ride it out through the down times? Who will successfully navigate the road to the Next Economy? In other words, which companies will be nimble enough to react to market conditions, and which will end up as roadkill along the way?

Our research clearly shows that the strongest companies adhere to a combination of the enduring leadership principles, detailed in Part I based on our studies of top CEOs, along with the 6 factors for successful execution, examined in Part II. Each company will find different ways to weave these tenets together. Some emphasize speed, while others focus on customer feedback. Sometimes it's hard to distinguish among the principles because they are so tightly interwoven. But these rules of the road are certainly the pillars that support a successful business strategy and structure in a tech-driven world.

To examine how a company can successfully combine these principles and strategies, let's take a look under the hood of General Electric's storied success. If you scrutinize the company's growth hard enough, each of the success factors begins to emerge clearly—and make sense.

C A S E   S T U D Y

General Electric
Executing Is in the Corporate DNA

At General Electric, the 6 principles work because people throughout the organization—at all levels—make them work. The impetus for GE to become Web-centric has been driven both the top down and the bottom up.

The top-down initiative officially began in sunny Boca Raton, Florida. At what has become known as a watershed meeting in the company's history in January 1999, then-chairman Jack Welch assigned all his business unit presidents the mandate to accelerate their Internet strategies. But rather than simply asking them to develop e-commerce business plans, the way most corporate managers would do, he phrased the assignment quite differently. "You have 90 days to figure out a way that a dot.com can destroy your business. And get there first." The business-planning process that resulted came to be known as "Destroy-your-business.com."

The way the question itself was posed forced the division presidents and their teams to take risks and develop aggressive approaches to their business strategy. Welch also gave them a short fuse—90 days—to get the company moving rapidly, and held them accountable for delivering. Not surprisingly, every GE business hit the deadline.

Rather than hire an army of consultants, Welch and his chief information officer, Gary Reiner, concluded that GE's employees knew their businesses well enough and that the Internet was not so complicated that they could not execute this assignment themselves. In all, according to Reiner, GE dedicated about 1,000 employees out of a workforce of 34,000 to the initial business effort. And 80% of those were regular GE employees who learned the Web. The focus was on using internal resources as opposed to recruiting heavily from the high-tech world, the more common corporate approach.

That directive from the chairman is typical of how things are done at GE. Find an overarching theme, make it the company's top priority, and drive it through the company rapidly, holding people accountable for successful execution.

It works at GE because rallying around a single priority and executing successfully is part of the company's culture—it's in the gene pool, as they say. And over his two decades at the helm of the world's most admired company, Welch masterfully galvanized folks around one big initiative after another. Another key, of course, was selecting the right theme at the right time and then *sticking with it* for long enough to make it a normal part of the company's operations, organization, and culture. This is far easier said than done: It's hard to find common ground between NBC and GE Capital, or GE

Lighting and GE Power Systems—and there are just four of the company's top 20 businesses. So the initiatives must be broad enough
yet relevant enough to impact them all.

Welch's big initiatives often set the course not just for his company but for much of corporate America. Consider Welch's objective
to be "number one or two in your industry," or the push to tear down
organizational boundaries, or the Six Sigma quality program, or the
rapid expansion into e-business. These objectives—and even the
language used to describe them—have become part of the currency
of American business.

So how have these initiatives translated into numbers? Under
Welch's term, GE grew from $28 billion in revenue and $13 billion in
market value in 1981 when he was appointed CEO, to $130 billion in
2000 revenue and $500 billion in market value. These compound
annual growth rates of 8% in revenue and 21% in market value sub-
stantially outperform the 6% for the growth of the U.S. economy
overall and the 11% growth in the S & P 500.

The numbers make sense when you see how these large themes
move into action. Once the company's mandate is received from on
high, implementation works both from the top down and the bottom up. Since one of GE's particular strengths is a flat organization
structure, where only four layers separate the top and bottom of
any business unit, changes can bubble up fairly quickly. Of course,
this flat structure is another of the ways that change is able to oc-
cur faster at GE than at many smaller companies. Change comes
from two directions at once.

Gary Reiner, who in addition to serving as GE's chief information
officer is the de facto "e-Business czar," explains to us how all this
works in practice.

Nothing in a company is going to change unless employees buy
in. It is that simple. At GE, this has been an important part of the
success of its e-Business initiative.

"The majority of people at GE are loving the e-Business initiative," Reiner explains. "I don't mean liking it, I mean loving it. They are feeling that this was over-due and sorely needed. They believe it is something that will make all of our lives better. Even the minority of people who thought that we were already devoting *too much* time, effort, and money to e-Business and information technology have now bought in. They have seen our success. They have seen the speed at which we have changed and improved. And they have now really bought in."

"The average customer inquiry handled online costs us 20 cents. The average offline cost of that same call going through an answer center, for one of our low-tech products, is $5. And in these products businesses, we have over 20 million phone calls per year. So the cost saving opportunity—about $96 million annually—was always apparent to us.

"What was less apparent until we got into it was the customer service that the Web could provide. This allows us to increase our productivity in how we deal with customers at the same time we increase our productivity on internal operations. Today, we have come to realize that the Web can be designed for both the revenue and cost sides of the business." —Gary Reiner, Chief Information Officer, GE

Since this is GE, stellar financial performance is vital. The company ties how rapidly it moves—our execution principle of going for speed—to the company's bottom-line performance.

"In our experience at GE, very strong performance is driven by two things," Reiner says. "Customer productivity—improvements in the way we deal with our customers, and internal productivity—improvements in the way we deal with ourselves. And there is no doubt our move to the Internet has paid off on both."

That payoff has been significant. In the year 2000, for example, e-business revenues for the company topped $11 billion, or nearly 10% of the company's total. Today, GE is perhaps the only major corporation to have transactional e-commerce capabilities in every one of its businesses. Cost savings through Internet productivity improvements in 2000 were estimated to be $400 million.

At the Boca Raton 2001 conference, a year after the dot.com crash on Wall Street, Welch once again addressed his top managers. Was his message to retreat from the e-Business priority? Exactly the opposite. The 2001 mandate: drive digitization and e-business to new heights within the company. The objective is now to identify $1.5 billion in cost savings activity directly related to its digitization efforts. In total, GE is eyeing opportunities to take out 20% to 30% of its corporate-wide sales, general and administrative costs (which total roughly $20 billion), in the coming years through e-business. For 2001 the company has projected that a stunning 15% of its total revenue, or $20 billion to $30 billion, will be generated online. In addition, 30% of procurement, or $15 billion of purchasing volume, is projected to be done online.

These massive numbers on both the revenue and cost sides are expected to grow even larger into the future as the Internet becomes increasingly woven into all of the company's operations and businesses.

SPEED AT GE IS NOT ONLY ABOUT TECHNOLOGY

At GE, speed is key beyond just technology development. It has also become the cornerstone, for example, of the company's recruiting efforts. "One of the things we've learned about college seniors, as well as graduate school students, is that they develop an immediate reaction to whatever they see, including how *we* respond when they first express an interest in the company," Reiner explains. "And so we've established cycle time rules in terms of how quickly we get back to an individual. We are giving our recruiters a certain amount of offers they can give on the spot, without having to go back to get approval. Because one of the things that I've found as I do recruiting, and I've done a lot, is that nothing impresses recruits more than in the immediate conclusion of an interview, offering them a job."

This story, obviously underscoring what GE has learned from the campus recruiting process, is interesting principally in the fact that it demonstrates how the company executes in ways that are obvious, but obvious only *after* you hear about them from someone else.

RISKY BUSINESS

Moving quickly is one thing. Managing risk is another. How does GE deal with the dilemma of protecting its existing channels of distribution, yet at the same time recognizing that if it does not cannibalize its business, someone else may? In other words, how does the "destroy-your-business.com" directive play out in practice?

"When we really decided to focus on the Internet in January of 1999, the question we asked was this: If someone was going to leverage the Internet to destroy our business, what would their economic model look like?" Reiner recalls. "In almost all cases, the answer was that we would be talking about a new market entrant coming at us, rather than an existing competitor. We figured that the existing competitor would have the same channel conflicts as we do. So we had to consider companies that did not suffer from that problem as seriously as our traditional competitors.

"Let's take retailers and our appliance business, for example. We knew that Whirlpool was not going to go around retailers and sell direct. Neither would Maytag. They couldn't afford to alienate the retailers. But who could potentially do this? It would be a company like Goldstar, which had a lot less to lose by going around the retail channel. So then we had to calculate what Goldstar's economics would be by selling direct and compare how that related to our economics."

That way GE could develop a business model that played to the company's strengths and helped offset its weaknesses. "The conclusion of our analysis was that the best approach for us would be a hybrid of going direct and working with our retail partners. In truth, it is $150 cheaper for us to build a refrigerator and get it to your home directly if you buy it on the Web than if we sell it to you in the traditional way. But if we could use the retailer's sales people, customer traffic and blend them with our warehousing and distribution scale, we could capture many of the benefits of going direct, and create a winning formula for our retailers at the same time."

The current GE Appliance arrangement with Home Depot demonstrates how this has come to work in practice. Prior to undertaking its Web effort, Home Depot was not a customer of GE Appliance. But in an effort to both test its new approach and to penetrate this major account, the company set up a Web-based system to arrange delivery of GE products to people who bought them at the giant retailer. GE's system, which is now in use in about 600 of Home Depot's 980 stores, lets salespeople enter a customer's order in the GE Appliance Web site and schedule delivery to the customer's home directly from a GE warehouse. GE Appliance handles installation. The Web site and fulfillment operation allowed GE Appliance to not only break into the Home Depot account but allowed it to become the *sole* appliance supplier to the home products giant.

The way GE determined how to use the Internet in the appliance business "is an example of a destroy-your-business.com analysis," Reiner says. "The issues of new market entrants, cannibalization, who captures what on the value chain were brought forward in our strategic reviews. So then the question becomes, what do you do about that? Do you wait for someone else to do it, or do you do it yourself?

"In most cases we found that the Internet was not going to be the vehicle for destroying our business. But it does—and will increasingly—put pressure on our businesses. The Internet therefore has forced us to rethink everything we do," Reiner adds.

Once a problem—or an opportunity such as saving $150 by selling direct—is identified, it is acted upon. Bureaucratic conflicts are not tolerated. That no-nonsense approach, Reiner says, is directly attributable to the way Jack Welch worked.

"He was extraordinarily good at doing things that made everybody aware of how serious he was about a particular initiative," Reiner says. "You can't underplay or underestimate that. He would replace someone who was doing well performance-wise, but who was not supporting the initiative. He'd do that publicly. We've all learned that one symbolic act is worth more than a million words. And the impact of removing that one guy is far bigger than that one guy who lost his job. It has an impact on the whole culture of the company."

This is a style that is embedded in the GE culture and it is already clear that it is continuing under the leadership of Welch's successor, Jeffrey Immelt.

That message—and any other the chairman wants to send—permeates the organization through what is known as the "operating system," the way GE "leverages the relationship between corporate headquarters and its individual businesses to reinforce initiatives and strategies," says Reiner.

"It starts in January, where the chairman lays out the goals for the year, and it works its way all the way through to the budgeting process in November for the following year. There's no way of getting around making progress on the key initiatives that the company wants to move forward on. All the interactions, all the people, the investment or expense spending—every aspect of it—is centered on what our goals are.

"The trick here though is to also pick people who get excited about what the objective is. That's the other side of the equation. It comes back to people, people, people," Reiner stresses. And, of course this whole way of doing business feeds on itself. An exciting strategy and the institutional ability to execute will attract the right people.

The strategy grows out of a healthy customer focus. GE is increasingly becoming an organization that can obsess the customer because it has the systems and people in place to react quickly to customer demand. "Successful companies have been incredibly customer focused long before the Internet was discovered," Reiner says. "Take a look at Home Depot or Wal-Mart. Of course, in Cisco's case, the Internet helped. But overall, the customer processes that they have in place are as much off-line as online.

"One can't argue with the fact that being customer obsessed is a secret to success," Reiner says. "It is not something that we have been particularly focused on as a company throughout most of our history, but we are moving in that direction right now. We are increasingly going to be rewarding people based on their customer focus and to be removing people based on their lack thereof. So it's something that we're moving aggressively towards. We're going to get there. We're not there yet, but we are heading there." Jeffrey Immelt, who earned his stripes across GE's Medical Systems, Plastics, and Appliance divisions culminating with the position of running GE Medical prior to being named CEO-elect in December 2000 and Chairman and CEO in September 2001, is particularly known to have a deep passion and commitment for customer satisfaction.

But a larger challenge for GE—and other companies born in the industrial age—is more fundamental. GE has a long tradition of standing behind its hard goods and making sure that everything runs nearly to perfection before it rolls off the production line. The process of assuring quality at this level has been honed over decades and is performed with scientific precision. For good reason: A jet engine, after all, mustn't freeze up once it's in action. At GE, there's a constant effort afoot to improve quality. It's known as Six Sigma, the intensive management process that is centered around having businesses have only six defects per 10,000 actions. GE has applied Six Sigma not only to manufacturing businesses, for which it was originally designed, but to service businesses. One example is NBC, which has implemented the approach to root out inefficiencies in its business affairs department, the unit that handles the network's deal-making operations.

But the world of software and the Internet is quite different from the industrial world. The Web engineering ethos says: Work fast and fix problems in later versions. (Microsoft, which has always rolled out products fast and furiously, admitting and fixing problems in later versions, turned this formula into an amazingly successful business process.) E-business executives often complain that it feels as if they are fixing the plane in midflight—an analogy that must sound terrifying to the jet engine engineers back at GE.

Reiner admits that this was a stumbling block for GE early on in its e-business initiatives. "So we had an issue, when the Internet initiative came along. There was a segment of the company that saw an inherent contradiction and was saying, 'Hey, you want us to be absolutely perfect, *and* yet you want us to go to launch quickly. Which do you want us to do?' My response was to say, 'Launch quickly on the Web with a very big "feedback button." Figure out to the greatest extent possible what the customer wants, and then get it out there and then be ready to change it. If you try to make it perfect by the time it got out, it wouldn't be, because things would have changed in such a way that you would be way behind what the market wants.' "

Today, GE has learned to balance—and somewhat integrate—the Six Sigma imperative against the demands of e-business technology. The result is a $110 billion company that learns quickly. And interestingly, Reiner says that some of the lessons learned in deploying Six Sigma actually made them more effective e-business leaders.

Reiner explains. "One of the things we learned from launching Six Sigma is that it is a mistake to bring people in to run the training process. When we initially launched Six Sigma in 1995 we said, 'we don't know much about this thing, we've got to go outside and hire a bunch of Six Sigma leaders for this.' When we did that we failed, because they didn't know which buttons to push within the organization. They didn't know where the clout was, they didn't know anything about our company, and basically we got nowhere.

"What we found was that it made more sense to take somebody from each business who knows a ton about the business, has a ton of credibility, knows which buttons to push, train them and hire some people from the outside to *support* them.

"We took that lesson with us as we pushed into e-Business. What we found was that about 20% of the people focused on e-Business should be hired from the outside, 80% from the inside." And there's one more key lesson here: Having the right folks in place is only half the battle. "We and a whole lot of other businesses are guilty of putting an internal process, such as a call center, on the Web, and keeping the existing process in place as well," Reiner says. "And we soon discovered that this was a bad idea. It's just a waste to have this duplicative effort. You've got to shut down the traditional process, and force all of your employees, encourage all of your customers, and somewhere between encourage and enforce our suppliers to move to the Web. And we are in the process of doing that everywhere right now."

A PUZZLEMENT

GE's actions make sense in hindsight. Of course, it didn't feel all that secure to executives as they lived through it. When everything you know is questioned and you are told to reinvent your business overnight, the common human reaction is increased heart rate and perspiration. Especially in a company like GE, where employee performance is plotted in five bands annually. The top two bands are rewarded handsomely, while those in the bottom tier are encouraged to leave.

So how does this company then encourage risk-taking and minimize the stresses that come with it? The GE answer is consistent with our principle for rewarding *appropriate* risk-taking. Again, Reiner explains:

"We try to distinguish between failure that is a marketing failure, and failure that comes from poor execution. And we try to keep the two very different. We do not penalize people for a market change, particularly if that market change was unforeseeable. We do penalize forecastable market changes that were ignored and, we penalize poor execution quickly."

Implicitly, this approach also involves absorbing uncertainty. If you know what your company values (and does not tolerate) it is easier to do your job day to day. Clearly, GE wants to remain a world-class company and measure up—or ahead of—the competition's efforts. "If someone is not growing his business as fast as the competition, that tells you something," says Reiner. "However, if someone is way ahead of the competition, but still didn't meet their stretch target, we wouldn't punish them for that. Those are two very different things."

Perhaps not surprisingly, the same focused attitude applies to the way the company executes deals and acquisitions—our sixth execution principle. "We do about a deal a day, mostly in GE Capital," Reiner says. "We are therefore able to have some great M&A skills in-house. Because we have top professionals whose full-time jobs are tax-related, negotiation-related, or legally-related, we have some extraordinarily talented people here at corporate. They have come here out of the top firms in their discipline. And they are exposed to something on the order of nine deals a day. So one of our great advantages is scale. We therefore don't need to go to the investment bankers, or the tax firms, in anywhere near the same degree as one would expect."

GE's tremendous deal capability does not always lead to the desired outcome, such as the attempt to acquire Honeywell. In October 2000, Honeywell had agreed to a merger of equals with

United Technologies, maker of Otis Elevators, Pratt & Whitney air-craft engines, and Sikorsky helicopters. But in an adrenaline-filled 48-hour time frame between the announcement of the Honeywell-United Technologies deal and joint board approval, GE put an offer together to top the bid. While the deal won the day with the United Technologies board, the speed failed to let the company do its homework on the regulatory front. Experts agree, however, that the exercise still demonstrated GE's deal-making skills.

GE takes its deal-making skills a step further in its digital econ-omy pursuits and—like Cisco and other leading companies—invests in the technology companies it will be buying products and services from.

"By early 1999, we knew we were going to be leveraging a whole lot of Internet-related products and buying a whole lot of software. So we decided that what made the most sense was to find businesses in the pre-IPO space and to give them bond commitments, in ex-change for equity prior to their IPO. It's a win/win, because they get to go on their road show saying that GE is a big customer of theirs. And we got the equity upside, as well as the services that we initially contracted for. The same strategy doesn't make sense with the way we deal with IBM, AT&T, or WorldCom. But it does make sense with a smaller company, where we can have a substantial impact on their equity ratio."

As the Welch era closes and the Immelt era begins, GE has de-veloped perhaps the most powerful execution capability of any com-pany in the traditional or new economies. And they've managed to evolve quickly from a world-class industrial power into a top-notch e-business firm. So even though the road to the Next Economy is marked by uncertainty, it's safe to assume that GE will only grow stronger for having made the journey.

CHAPTER 10

Implementing the 6 Success Factors for the Next Economy

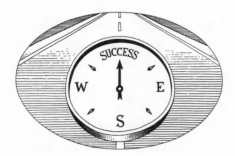

N othing recedes like success," the legendary newspaper columnist Walter Winchell once observed. For those who've recently
left fallen dot.coms, the words resonate all too harshly. During
the holiday season at the end of 2000, the *New York Times* grabbed
for an apt pop culture metaphor: "the online retailing business was
looking like the last episodes of *Survivor."*

The ups and downs of Internet companies (mostly the downs
starting from mid-2000) have been prominently chronicled in the
media. *Fortune* magazine maintains its "Dot.com death toll" feature
keeping a biweekly count of Internet company closings (latest toll
for 2001—303 as of September 17, 2001). Others ranging from as
respectable a vehicle as *The Wall Street Journal Interactive Edition* to
a prominent Web site with a name not suitable for publication (okay,

you have to fill in the two missing letters, f—kedcompany.com) have also been tallying the cost of the former irrational exuberance driving the market.

Does this mean that the Internet is dead? Was the whole thing just a fad? Can we finally get back to normal?

Of course not.

While our national attention has shifted from the certainty of taking an e-commerce company from idea to IPO and making millions in the process, to the aftermath of the bust, where some observers have pronounced the whole Internet phenomenon DOA, the reality is somewhere in between. There have indeed been some great entrepreneurial success stories. And there have also been many true stories of entrepreneurs and investors who lost everything. The fact is that the entrepreneurial process was never that easy. Though there were an excess of Internet companies that got funded (irresponsibly) and were taken public (prematurely), the process was demanding and took zealous devotion to a concept and brutal work hours. And for those who made it, only a sliver ever realized any serious financial gains. This messy process, however, did breed a smattering of companies that will flourish in the new century, hopefully including those chronicled in this book.

The reality is that how we communicate is inextricably linked to how the world does business. The entrepreneurial process has catalyzed a tsunami of economic development directly related to our heightened pace of communication. A little historical perspective vividly illustrates the point.

According to Ted Lewis's analysis in his book *The Friction-Free Economy*, economic development over human history has accelerated as the rate of interpersonal interaction has increased. And as the table on page 207 demonstrates, the acceleration has occurred neatly, increasing 10-fold times per "age."

For additional perspective, let's look at the evolution of the telephone. At the end of 1877, the first year the Bell Telephone

Age	Length of Time (years)	Rate of Interaction (mph)	Time to Circle Earth (years)
Agrarian Age	3,000–5,000	3–5 (Human)	3–5 (Years)
Industrial Revolution	300–500	3–50 (Horse-Auto)	0.3–0.5 (Months)
Post-Industrial	3–50	300–500 (Airliner)	0.03–0.05 (Days)
Digital (or Friction-Free)	3–5	3,000–5,000 (Network)	0.003–0.005 (Hours)

Company sold telephone equipment and service, there were roughly 3,000 phones in the country, or 1 per every 10,000 people. In part, this was because the Bell Telephone Company believed that the business segment (B-to-B as it would be known today) was a better and more profitable channel than the consumer segment (today's B-to-C). With this in mind, the Bell Telephone Company sold telephones to American businesses at an amazing rate: 60,000 by the end of 1880 and 250,000 by the end of 1893, the last year of their 16-year patent-backed monopoly.

Here's where the story takes on some familiar shades: By the turn of the 20th century, thousands of start-up telephone companies had sprung up to serve the needs of farmers, tradesmen, remote locations, and other markets that Ma Bell hadn't captured. By 1902 approximately 9,000 such start-ups existed and by 1920, there were more than 13 million phones in the country, or roughly 123 for every 1,000 people.

Imagine if you were to condense that period of 43 years into 6, triple the number of start-up companies, and then multiply the number of phones by 9. *Voilà!* What you'd have is the evolution of the digital economy.

The pace of Internet adoption has far outstripped any preceding technology; nothing even comes close. It took less than 5 years for 50 million people to log onto the Internet around the world. By comparison, to achieve this same level of penetration, it took television 13 years, while radio took an even longer 38 years. In the past 4 years, the number of Internet hosts has increased 6-fold, and the number of domain names has increased more than 30-fold. Internet traffic doubles every 100 days with little sign yet of slowing down. Today, there are over 100 million Internet users in the United States and electronic commerce accounted for over $100 billion in sales during 1999, more than double the amount in 1998. As for the number of companies, no one really knows how many budding ventures are still up and running waiting to prove their business model. What we do know is that there are a lot of them, more than we could have ever imagined in 1893—or even 1993.

Now think about the next generation of schoolchildren for a moment. As a trustee of my alma mater, Vassar College, I attend regular quarterly meetings. Recently, the vice president of information technology shared the results of the Fall 2000 Student Computing Survey. The study (which is surely consistent with most colleges and universities around the country) revealed that 93% of Vassar students now own their own computers, 99% of the students use e-mail regularly, and 97% use the Internet for research. More amazingly, the study divulged that half of the students spend two to five hours online every day and 14% spend more than five hours each day online. Once the intoxicating allure of instant communications and unlimited information has been experienced by these future leaders of society, there will be no turning back.

Similar studies of younger children, ages two to 17, suggest that America's youngsters spend more than four and a half hours in front of a television, computer, or video game screen each day. While television still accounts for 20 to 25 hours of use a week for children, more and more children turn to the Internet before they flip on the television. This is not all that surprising. After all, more American families own a television set than own a telephone, and 43% of American households have computers with Internet access at home.

Our children are setting a highly credible example of how communications and information technology will be used in the Next Economy. They are multitasking with their computers, often darting from one activity to another, and they are plugged in at every level. They download music, have real-time chats with each other, schedule activities, keep up extended personal networks, buy-sell-trade and auction everything from Pokeman cards to bikes, and they do all of this while listening to music, playing video games, and often, much to our chagrin, doing their homework. If our companies could only attempt to implement IT strategies as complex and integrated as our teenagers, corporate technology usage would be up dramatically.

Clearly, the Internet is not a fad. It is time to get back to work and reemphasize how to use it to thrive in the Next Economy. And that is the point of this concluding chapter, in which we take each of the 6 success factors from the Business Execution Wheel and examine their implementation.

SUCCESS FACTOR #1: GO FOR SPEED

Think back to the days before cell phones. E-mail. Voice mail. Laptops. Overnight delivery. Although this time is less than two decades ago, it is difficult for most people to remember how work got done.

Speed is relative. It's something we adjust to so well that we have a hard time even imagining what we did when everything was mimeographed or worse, handwritten and sent in a regular envelope for three- to six-day delivery by the trusty postman. Speed today is a requirement for success. Those who can't get a proposal out quickly may lose out to a competitor and speed also begets even more speed. The performance bar is constantly raised. Once you've crashed through one proposal, the client expects the next one to come even faster and have richer insights.

As James Gleick reported in his book, *Faster: The Acceleration of Just About Everything,* speed has become an obsession. "The more time you have on your hands the less important you must be. So sleep in the office. Never own up to an available lunch slot." After all, who are the people who need handheld computers and cell phones? People with no time. But Gleick alludes to some of the negative consequences which companies must consider in our quest for ever accelerating speed. As he points out, decisions can ferment during slow periods. "We may need to set aside formal time for deliberation, where once we used accidental time."

Have you ever pressed the Send button on your e-mail, only to regret your impulse a nanosecond later? Has your management team ever complained about spending all day in meetings that other people scheduled using meeting organizer software?

As a company works to create organizational speed, it is important to remember that people and organizations have their limitations. A culture which reveres speed should also allow room for down time, thoughtful decision-making, and review.

With that in mind, let's review and elaborate on the 10 ways to implement the success factor of speed, listed at the end of "Go for Speed" (page 46):

1. *Be first to market—or a smart and fast follower.* The reality is that few companies can be first to market, and many successful companies or products are quite late. However, that does not mean that the company or division shouldn't strive to be first as often as possible and make a point of celebrating these occasions. Everyone likes to come in first and investors and employees may

not stay for the end of the race if they believe your company is the tortoise. That said, there are also great examples of fast or smart followers, such as Microsoft, which learned from others' experiences. Sometimes companies can gain an important advantage by watching others struggle with problems and thereby avoid costly and time-consuming trial and error. The advantages of being a smart follower in today's difficult market environment are clear. The fact still remains, however, that even as a smart follower, companies have to move fast and adjust incredibly quickly. Speed is therefore at the heart of all successful enterprises riding into the Next Economy.

2. *Set up simple but executable business modules.* Simple things work well. Think about a strategy in terms of a system of component parts, or modules. eBay executes this principle beautifully by breaking its business into easy-to-understand pieces and then developing and executing a strategy for each module.

3. *Show people the corporate map.* Too often, many employees do not know the true structure of the company. If you have to get something done, it helps to have not only an organizational chart but a real guidebook of how things operate and who is accountable for what. Find out which people in the organization know how the company is *really* structured and have them work on a road map for others, especially for new employees.

4. *Flatten the company.* Organizational layers are essential, but too many of them can stifle your ability to innovate and move quickly. By breaking down the hierarchical layers, you broaden accountability. Yahoo!, for example, pushes accountability far down the organizational pyramid; GE's rule of thumb is to have no more than four layers between the head of a business unit and the entry-level employee. If a business gets too large or complex, it may be time to restructure the business into smaller business units.

5. *Share the vision.* What is special about your company and where

do you want to take it? What mantra can you use to rally support? It is not always enough just to talk about it: If you *do* walk the talk and don't evangelize, then nobody will know. The best leaders repeat the mantra so often that it soon becomes second nature to everyone in the company. They have learned that even if they feel that they are being redundant, people on the other end of the communication may need to hear the same vision three, four, or even five times before it really starts to sink in. Think of your audience, not yourself.

6. *Measure and reward speed.* Like everything else, you need to reward speed in order to encourage it. Yet you need to do so in a way that does not promote recklessness. This can only be done effectively by coming up with ways to measure how quickly things should be done. As the GE case study demonstrates, it is possible to quantify and measure even "soft" things, such as NBC's business affairs process. As Peter Drucker famously wrote, "What gets measured, gets managed."

7. *Let technology aid communications—not take it over.* I would surmise that for every three steps forward gained through e-mail, most people take one step backward due to misunderstandings. Speed of communication cannot replace quality. Technology is not always the answer, whether you are communicating in-house with your staff or your boss, or whether you are communicating with clients and customers.

8. *Analyze your company's path of decision-making.* Have you ever wondered what needs to happen in order to replace a printer? Or buy an expensive piece of software? How about recruiting a new employee to a divisional management team or putting together a proposal to woo a new customer? Is decision-making in your company like finding your way through an arcane maze? If so, look for shortcuts that will eliminate extra layers and give employees more autonomy to make decisions.

9. *Think 24/7.* In an age of truly global business, it is important to

remember that time is a frame of reference which is dependent on the person or company in question. The more diverse your supplier, customer, and partner base, the more creative you have to be in operating a 24/7 business. Outsourcing, unconventional work hours, and other organizational changes can help stretch your organization beyond 9 to 5.

10. *Lead by example.* In *Lessons from the Top*, we stressed the importance of leading by example. In the case of speed, leaders need to be accessible and able to make rapid decisions. If you are perceived to be unresponsive or slow to act, you will have an uphill battle in trying to sell the need to speed things up in your organization. If you find that you are a bottleneck for certain operations or decisions, find a way to step aside.

Speed, of course, is only one element of the Business Execution Wheel. It needs the other elements for your company to most effectively and powerfully work.

SUCCESS FACTOR #2: CREATE A LEARNING ORGANIZATION

Popularized over a decade ago by Peter Senge's classic book *The Fifth Discipline*, organizational learning has been a cornerstone of many organizations' strategies for some time now. Implementing knowledge management systems, corporate intranets, training programs, and other much touted facilitators of organizational learning has become common across many organizations, large and small. As the key value of an organization shifts from physical to intellectual capital, improving your company's ability to learn is the historical equivalent of building grain silos and developing inventory tracking systems.

Unfortunately, many executives have become the victim of one of the most common "learning" traps: the *illusion* of knowledge. It is a concern Socrates first addressed in describing how the Egyptian god who invented letters, Thoth, was criticized by Thamus, King of Egypt:

> This discovery of yours [letters] will create forgetfulness in the learners' souls, because they will not use their memories; they will trust to the external written characters and not remember of themselves. The specific which you have discovered is an aid not to memory, but to reminiscence, and you give your disciples not truth, but only the semblance of truth; they will be hearers of many things and will have learned nothing; they will appear to be omniscient and will generally know nothing; they will be tiresome company, having shown the wisdom without the reality.

When was the last time you sent a memo or typed critical information into a database when your better instincts told you that you really should have had a face-to-face or person-to-person conversation? Knowledge systems or tools cannot be substituted for knowledge itself. As one teacher I know remarked, "My students used to read. Now they download the relevant passage from a website and believe they have finished the assignment."

What follows is an elaboration on the 10 ways to implement the success factor of learning at the end of "Create a Learning Organization."

1. *Shorten feedback cycles.* George Bernard Shaw once suggested that "The only person who behaves sensibly is my tailor. He takes new measurements every time he sees me. All the rest go on with their old measurements." You need to be responsible to the business environment and those around you, not in three-year time spans, but constantly. Don't rely on one or two means of research, whether it is customer-, client-, or employee-centered. Break up your process into shorter iterative cycles.

2. *Transfer knowledge.* Without informal and formal teaching and mentoring, you will never have transfers of knowledge on the

level you need within your organization. Look for opportunities or processes that will encourage learning. Create a culture of learning that pervades everything that you do.

3. *Expand the company's "listening circles."* Often, executives listen too infrequently, and when they do, they listen to the wrong people. At formal meetings, people tend to "posture"—it is unlikely that you will hear what is really going on. Walk the halls, engage those above and below you in informal ways. Stop by a colleague's office and ask him or her how things are going. If someone is working on a new project, ask if you can help (a great way to probe the progress of an initiative or the resource allocation). Sam Walton, the founder of the world's largest retail chain, Wal-Mart, once flew to Texas, flagged down a Wal-Mart truck, and rode for over 100 miles to "chat with the driver." Remember, there is no such thing as a small customer or an unimportant employee. Everyone matters and most people have ideas you should know about.

4. *Focus on what is really going on rather than just on appearances.* Robert Pirsig suggested that the world appears different from a motorcycle than through a car window. By changing your perspective and trusting what you see, you will learn more. Leonardo da Vinci wrote that, "Experience does not ever err, it is only your judgment that errs in promising itself results which are not caused by your experiments." Focusing on the real outcome of an action is critical to ensuring that you are moving in the right direction.

5. *Measure the right things to support learning.* Spend as much time making sure you are measuring the right things as you do measuring them. As we become more addicted to measurement, keep in mind the link between measurement and performance. Resist the temptation to rely on gut or instinct with regard to qualitative issues. As The Motley Fool illustrated with its "happiness index," great companies find a

way to measure even so-called soft issues, such as culture and quality.

6. *Reward teaching and learning.* Learning is not just about gaining a certification or improving performance. If you do not reward learning, and the teaching that enables it, then you will not instill it as an organizational necessity. I was touched by a story of a schoolteacher near the end of her career who asked for a computer in her room only to be told that she didn't need one because she probably wouldn't use it. The teacher fought for the computer and won. Initially, she didn't know what to do with it, but as she learned what it could be used for, she began creating whole new lessons for her kids, which were later praised by other teachers, parents, and eventually the local Board of Education. Without the computer, she could never have explored this new realm of possibilities. If you want people to be proactive, then you will need to make sure they are, as Fred Lazarus, the former Chairman of the Federated Department Stores, said, "curious as to what makes the whole business tick and have the ambition and desire to fight to get to a place of more responsibility."

7. *Study and remember history.* As Winston Churchill remarked, "Study history, study history; in history lies all the secrets. . . ." Keep an organizational and personal archive. First, take time to archive e-mails, letters, and other important documents so you can learn from and pass along your own "history." Next, learn about the people who were in your position before you (assuming there were any) and about the history of your division, the company, and the product or service you are working on. Next, broaden your reach. Identify others who have been in similar situations and learn how they handled themselves. If you consider yourself not only the captain but the designer of your destiny, there is much you can learn from.

8. *Encourage employees' activities outside of their jobs.* Nothing is as important as promoting learning—in all forms. It is a topic

worth special mention because it is too often lost in our hectic business world. Those who participate in diverse activities when they are not at work are more creatively and emotionally recharged when they are at work. As Arthur Koestler wrote in *The Act of Creation,* "Creative Synthesis is the sudden interlocking of two previously unrelated skills, or matrices of thought." Whether or not any particular pursuit leads to a breakthrough innovation, it helps make for a much more stimulating and exciting workplace. So encourage someone to take time off to pursue other interests and encourage them to share that experience with those around them.

9. *Assess each learning initiative in the context of your organizational culture to ensure effectiveness.* Learning is a difficult thing to assess, and much research has pointed this out. Determine your audience. Decide which people in your company are your first movers, those who are followers, and those who are observers. Next, assess the goals for each audience with each initiative. Were first-movers excited? Did the followers feel motivated? Did the observers (internal or external) feel something positive taking place?

10. *Acknowledge others' efforts to change.* Take the time to tell everyone about the impact they are having. If you are asking people to learn new skills, then you need to include them in presentations about how the business is doing and what you want the future to look like. Don't leave individuals or groups out. Learn to give, rather than take, credit.

SUCCESS FACTOR #3: OBSESS THE CUSTOMER

In the 1960s, Procter & Gamble installed an 800 number for customers. They quickly learned that lots of consumers were doing more loads of laundry and in more varied temperatures because of the introduction of new fabrics. In response, P&G launched a new product, All Temperature Cheer. Since this early experiment with customer feedback, countless products, services, and processes have been created and implemented by companies around the world to get a better handle on what their customers really want.

These days, obsessing about your customer can be less obvious than it seems. Here is an elaboration of 10 ways to execute the success factor of customer obsession outlined at the end of "Obsess the Customer."

1. *Find out who your customer really is.* Too often, a product or service is designed around a mythical customer. Take the time to measure more than who the most common consumer of your offering is. Who is buying it first? Who is most influential in telling other customers about your product or service? Who is using what you designed in new ways? Geraldine Laybourne, founder and Chairman of Oxygen Media and former President of Nickelodeon, was notorious for using customer research in developing programming for kids at Nick. "The key to Nick's success over the years has been that we talked to kids in their own language, we didn't talk down to them or patronize them. Our ability to do this came directly out of rigorous research, in which we continually met with, spoke to, and more importantly listened to our customers—kids." This is especially important in more political corporate environments, where it is easy to start describing your customers in ways that you want them described. How often have you seen so-called industry experts proclaiming trends evidenced only within their own minds? Go out on the road or on the Web and interact. Measure not only the averages, but the individual.

2. *Create a big comments box on your Web site.* Do you have a comments box on your Web site, in your stores, or in your office? Take the time to put it there *and assign people to read what comes*

through it. When possible, respond not only to the people who gave you comments but to their requests as well.

3. *Show appreciation for your customers' loyalty by saying thank you.* In *Leadership Is an Art,* Max Dupree wrote, "The last responsibility of a leader is to say thank you." This bit of advice is included in almost every business advice book, yet few people follow it. If in doubt, just thank people. If you have a hard time remembering what they did that is worth thanking them for, then perhaps you are overthinking the rule. Many executives have developed strong loyalty from others just by thanking them for sending an e-mail or returning a call. You can easily extend this principle throughout your organization, but don't forget to thank your customers as well. They don't need to be shopping from you or hiring you or listening to you.

4. *Manage customer information.* In an age of massive relational databases, it is amazing to witness the wide delta between organizations that obsess about customer data and those that don't. Consider what is important to know about them. Find ways to use the information you gather after you know your customers well. But be extremely respectful of your customers' privacy. Just because they gave you data easily doesn't mean they expect you to share it or use it irresponsibly. Ironically, the legal standards of online or electronic usage of such data is becoming more strict than offline practices. What sort of privacy practices do you have?

5. *Give customers what they want.* Many great companies have disappeared over time. Have you ever wondered what happened to companies that built horse-drawn carriages, manufactured vacuum tubes or phonographs? Today, while some companies have been amazing at transforming themselves into just-in-time production facilities, for example, others have plodded on as they did before. As Gary Hamel and C. K. Prahalad suggest in *Competing for the Future,* "A company can control its own destiny

only if it understands how to control the destiny of its industry. To do so, it must change in some fundamental way the rules of an industry." Listening to your customers—and not only your most common or profitable customers—is one of the ways to ensure that you can escape being controlled by the reactions of everyone else in your industry and be able to reinvent yourself.

6. *Don't neglect viral marketing.* All of a sudden, business gurus have been focusing a lot of attention on viral marketing in association with the Internet. Viral marketing isn't all that new, of course, it's just word-of-mouth marketing done on the Web. Getting people to talk about your product happens by doing the right things right. But you also need to know when the wrong things are getting done too. People are notoriously good at gossip and they will do so whether they are spreading the virtues of your product or not. We have not yet seen anyone mount a good viral marketing campaign around a product no one likes, or for a company that betrays the trust of its consumers. If you find that there just isn't any "buzz" around your product or service, it's likely that either no one knows about it, or that no one cares, because it is not special enough. You may love your product. Unfortunately, what *you* think doesn't matter as much as what your customers think.

7. *Be sincere.* Don't worry so much about telling your customers you care—worry about *caring.* If everyone in your company truly believes that they are part of making a difference, then you have won a crucial battle in this regard. We have all witnessed the empty corporate mission statement proclaiming "The Customer Is Always Right" hanging over a customer service counter with a line that never seems to move. If your Web site takes orders, then you should take returns as well. If your database sends out thank-you cards to customers, don't forget to tell them about product improvements they helped initiate. If you remember that your company is really just a group of people working to-

gether trying to do the best they can, then each one of your customers should recognize that there is a real person working to make their experience better.

8. *Keep things simple.* The difficulty of many start-ups and the resulting corporate response to them is that people begin to define their products, companies, or services in hyperbole. How many times have you heard that a particular Web site is the leading destination for everyone to do everything all the time? Tell it like it is, and if in doubt, repeat yourself.

9. *Personalize everything you can.* Recent studies suggest that most people prefer a personalized experience online. Web sites claim that they offer a personalized experience. But how many companies can claim the same thing? Take a lesson from the Web: Collect a little more information from everyone your company interacts with so that you can use that information to make your next interaction with them more positive. Doesn't it make you feel warm inside when you check into a hotel you've stayed at and they greet you by name and say, "Welcome back"?

10. *Be obsessive about the customer experience.* If you tell a person something that is true and something that is a lie or an exaggeration, they will remember the lie. If you tell customers you care and then make it difficult to use your product or service, you are wasting your efforts. Make each time you interact with a customer an opportunity to exceed their expectations. As Andy Grove, chairman of Intel, would say, be *paranoid* about your customers and their business. Too many companies believe that online, people expect less, when in fact, they often expect more.

SUCCESS FACTOR #4: REWARD (APPROPRIATE) RISK-TAKING AND FAILURE

An e-business, by its very nature, is filled with a certain amount of risk. As Amazon's Jeff Bezos said: "I don't want to give the impression that our future success is assured. I believe the opposite. I believe our future success is *not* assured. If you look at the history of pioneers, it's not good." Despite this, if a company or an individual just plays it safe, failure is all but assured. The bottom line is that every company must take risks. More important, it is the reinforcing behavior that goes along with those decisions that usually helps promote positive rather than negative risk-taking. To compete in new uncharted territories, companies must measure managerial performance differently. Too often, when appraising the performance of a manager, the risk associated with the manager's objective is often overlooked in favor of focusing on performance. As a result, a manager who loses money running a business with a 20-year history of profitable growth is treated the same as a manager who loses money pursuing a new space. When new ventures hold real risk for employees, then the best managers won't want to manage the riskiest and often most important ventures for a company unless risk is rewarded differently. Smart risk-taking should be rewarded. Doing nothing can prove to be the riskiest.

Here is an elaboration of the 10 ways to reward risk-taking noted in the "Reward (Appropriate) Risk-Taking and Failure" chapter.

1. *Set up experiments, not contests.* If you set up risk-taking as competitions, then 50% of your company will always feel like losers. If you set up risk-taking as an experiment, then 100% of your company can feel like discoverers. Competitive energy can be highly motivating, but you must recognize the consequences of associating risk-taking with winning or losing. Make learning—not winning—the objective.

2. *Mitigate personal and organizational risk.* Few will admit that they actually enjoy risky or uncertain environments. In fact, uncertainty contributes greatly to stress and is a major reason for many people leaving their jobs. If you think you have a risky but winning strategy, find a way to mitigate the risk. In financial markets, this notion is called hedging.

3. *Encourage creative destruction.* Economist Joseph Schumpeter coined the phrase *creative destruction* early in the 20th century, in his work *Capitalism, Socialism and Democracy.* "The same process of industrial mutation—if I may use that biological term—that *incessantly* revolutionizes the economic structure *from within,* instantly destroying the old one, incessantly creating the new one. This process of Creative Destruction is the essential fact about capitalism." Later promoted by others including Peter Drucker, Lester Thurow, and Richard Nolan, creative destruction acknowledges that organizational structures and objectives must change to make way for new ones. If there is no transformation within a firm, then companies, particularly entrepreneurial ones, will bring about more competition. The firms that have succeeded best at changing to an intellectual asset base have best been able to re-create their businesses.

4. *Identify and support risk-takers.* Every company has a natural aversion or affinity for risk. The same holds true for every person. It is critical to align those within an organization who are the most inclined to negotiate risk to those projects and areas that require risk-taking. And sometimes it is the most traditional areas of a company that need a risk-taker. Conversely, you must align those who are not inclined toward risk to areas of the organization that best suit them. To keep a company in balance in terms of risk, make sure that you are staffed with the right composition of employees. Is your company characterized by 20% or 80% risk-takers? At a bare minimum, you need to know who your risk-takers are so that when you need to call them into action you can. If you can't find any or you can't keep any, then you need to create ways to make risk-takers more comfortable with the culture of your organization. As the GE case study so powerfully demonstrates, the culture and organizational processes that support risk-taking may need to shift to encourage more risk-taking and innovation.

5. *Eliminate politics by establishing a true meritocracy.* One of the

great lessons of the Internet "gold rush" was that a certain kind of skill and characteristic became more valuable than age, status, or even in some cases experience. This atmosphere should be seen as a wake-up call for companies to even out the internal playing fields so that each idea can be recognized for its merit, rather than for its source. Too often, when people feel that their career status hangs in the balance, they focus not on the business but on themselves. Make achievement the only way to move up or down in an organization, rather than "people posturing."

6. *Don't try to control everything.* To paraphrase Francis Bacon, if you begin with certainties you will end in doubt; if you begin in doubt, you may just end up in certainty. No matter how hard you try, you will be unable to be aware of, let alone control, everything. Those who try are fighting a losing battle that will serve only to fray their nerves and rob your management teams of tranquility.

7. *Ask people to make a difference.* If you asked the person sitting next to you in the office each day what he or she did for a living, what would the response be? If you asked yourself what your company intends to accomplish, what would be your answer? Too often, "changing the world" or "having a major, positive contribution on people" are not included in the everyday dialogue of business people. These motivating forces are often associated only with social or charitable causes. However, if your colleague replied by saying, "my job is to make this company the best place to work in the world," wouldn't that help motivate you? What if your company is trying to change the industry it competes in or create a new one altogether? Are you collectively changing the world? I would argue you are. Make sure everyone in your company realizes the seriousness, impact, and potential of the work they do. The minute they believe they just type reports or sell widgets is the minute you stop seeing any sign of risk-taking. It is not hard to see why this is the case. Few people will go out on a limb to type a report. But they might if they believe that report

will make the company the best place to work in the world and in turn set an example to inspire other companies—and people—to change.

8. *Encourage open and honest debate.* Encourage debate, but don't let it become personal or a contest. Casey Cowell, the cofounder of U.S. Robotics, believed that "where you want the contest is not among people, but among ideas." Encouraging intellectual risk-taking is one of the most important steps in promoting organizational risk-taking. In today's economy, almost all employees are measured not on their physical strength but on their intellectual prowess. Thus, an atmosphere that enables individuals to open their minds creatively with others is a place where people feel that their ideas are valued.

9. *Challenge old methods.* Don't do everything the way it has always been done—challenge old methods. That doesn't mean you should destroy good ways of doing things just because they have been around for a while. However, it is important to encourage new ways of doing things and experimenting with new ideas. George Bernard Shaw wrote that "Reasonable people adapt themselves to the world. Unreasonable people attempt to adapt the world to themselves. All progress, therefore, depends on unreasonable people." Don't be reasonable all the time.

10. *Watch your competitors for signs of change and be ready to act.* Your competition may not always be right, but don't assume that they are wrong. If other companies are adopting something new, or your competitors are offering new or different services or products, investigate them. Who in your company is responsible for watching the competition? On the one hand, the answer should be everyone, but on the other, there should be a formal competitive monitoring system.

SUCCESS FACTOR #5: ABSORB UNCERTAINTY

People have always wanted to predict the future so that they can eliminate most uncertainty from their lives. We have never liked uncertainty. As Vernon A. Walters, the former U.S. Ambassador to the United Nations and the Federal Republic of Germany, suggested, "Let them think. Worry. Wonder. Uncertainty is the most chilling thing of all." If the job of a leader is to be the captain of the ship, then it is also his or her job to steady the sea.

A president of a major consulting firm added, "Change has considerable psychological impact on the human mind. To the fearful, it is threatening because it means that things may get worse. To the hopeful, it is encouraging because things may get better. To the confident, it is inspiring because the challenge exists to make things better. Obviously, then, one's character and frame of mind determine how readily he brings about change and how he reacts to change that is imposed on him." As a manager, it is vital that you be regarded as a confident person in the organization and inspire that confidence in others.

Here is an elaboration of the 10 ways to implement the success factor of absorbing uncertainty, noted in the "Absorb Uncertainty" chapter:

1. *Take action!* Avoid overanalysis, and come up with a decision. Most people feel more comfortable after a decision is made than before, so don't make a habit of keeping people waiting.

2. *Don't unleash change all at once—start slowly and build momentum.* Most people are not naturally comfortable with uncertainty. They don't welcome constant change as it tends to resemble uncertainty. Manage the stress of change by trying to create periods of stability. When change is necessary, remember even a mountain must be climbed one step at a time. Often the first

step is the hardest. When people start seeing the impact of their efforts, they are motivated to redouble their commitment. It is that kind of commitment that can take the organization to the next level. Remember, most people respond well to positive feedback—the kind that comes from quick wins.

3. *Be visible.* In difficult times or periods of crisis, people look to their leaders to fill the void and for signals to help them gauge how to react. In wartime, presidents and prime ministers often make national television addresses to put dangers in context. So too in business. After the Wall Street crash in October 1987, for example, the senior leadership of Goldman Sachs held repeated firmwide conference calls to calm the fears of shaken professionals—so they could calm the fears of their clients.

4. *Remind those who work for you that anxiety is natural in an uncertain situation.* People like to know where they are going, and setting a straight organizational path certainly helps. Remind people that no one really knows where the future economy is heading and that you cannot afford to be overly precise in such dynamic times. The more rigid your heading, the less likely you will be able to absorb the uncertainty of the journey. Encourage people that while it is natural to feel anxious, they'll feel better if they can let go to a degree.

5. *Let people know how your plans affect them.* If you are like most people, when you hear weather or traffic reports, you usually do a quick comparison to see if you will be affected. If you determine that you won't, you tune out. Most people feel the same way about abstract concepts like corporate mission statements. If you can show people what it means for them, they won't tune out or feel left behind.

6. *Keep everyone involved, but make sure that participation in change initiatives is a matter of choice.* Make sure everyone feels involved and part of the team, but remember that passion is a key ingredient in change. Being sensitive to who is motivated by change

will go a long way toward reducing the uncertainty that people feel in transitional times. Some people love the glory of creating something new and being recognized publicly by their peers; others work hard while they are at work but are committed to getting home to their children at a reasonable hour.

7. *Be open, rather than secretive.* There is nothing more disconcerting than being kept in the dark. Most people would rather know the cause of their malady than suffer the same symptoms without knowing why. In turbulent times, people appreciate being kept informed so that they can try to anticipate what is coming down the road. Be consistent with the amount of information that you share. Whenever possible, follow the principle of information transparency.

8. *Fix problems ahead of you, not behind you.* The past will always remain the same, whether you worry about it or not. If you spend your time fixated on the past, the present will certainly slip by.

9. *Don't let little things take over.* Make sure that people focus on the most important things. You only have enough time in the day to make a few decisions—make sure you focus on the big ones. An advertising executive was once telling a client all about his firm's process of internal approvals. The client listened for a few minutes and then said, "To be honest, I trust that you have a great process to make sure you like an ad campaign. Just remember that the more time you spend making sure you like it, the less time you will have to change it if I don't." Make sure you can distinguish between the little things and the big things, and don't let people consume themselves with the little ones.

10. *When you change your mind, admit it.* "Remember that to change thy mind and to follow him that sets thee right, is to be none the less the free agent that thou wast before," commented Marcus Aurelius Antoninus, A.D. 188–217. Everyone appreciates someone who can admit they are wrong. If you change your mind, don't hide it.

SUCCESS FACTOR #6: MASTER DEAL-MAKING
AND PARTNERING

"From soup to nuts" is a term almost unheard of in business today. The era of the conglomerate is long gone and few companies (other than GE, perhaps) can claim to be world-class at unrelated businesses. Few executives can claim that they truly know their core competency enough to compete tomorrow. Because of that, deal-making and partnerships have become one of the core competencies that are essential to long-term success. The ultimate advantage is not to determine what your current competencies are, but which ones will be worth investing in and developing down the road.

Here are 10 ways to implement the success factor of deal-making, listed in the chapter "Master Deal-Making and Partnering."

1. *Figure out what you do well, and what you don't.* The first step in being able to form a successful partnership is to establish what you want to accomplish. This focus on what you want to make central to your organization was popularized by C. K. Prahalad and Gary Hamel in their book, *Competing for the Future* back in 1994. Decide what parts of your supply or service chain are holy ground—not to be given to others under any condition, and those parts for which you need as many helping hands as possible. One leading direct marketing company CEO concurred when he told me that his strategy was to "keep the brains in-house, but outsource the arms and legs."

2. *Don't let deals linger.* The only way to finalize a partnership is to complete them rather quickly. If you let them linger, competitors are often able to make a counteroffer, or if not, the natural momentum of a relationship becomes stale.

3. *Partnerships and deals need attention.* Signing a contract is only one point in a successful partnership. Sustainable partnerships

require hands-on attention. For less intensive deals such as affiliate sponsorship arrangements that means frequent reporting and an unobstructed information flow so that each party can regularly assess the value of the relationship.

4. *Make sure both parties benefit.* There is nothing as short-lived as a one-sided deal. Furthermore, if your partner fails or is under duress, it increases the chances that you will fail or share in the duress.

5. *Don't let prior relationships supersede your business objectives.* It is not uncommon to do a favor for a friend or former colleague. However, do not choose a partner because of a relationship when it would not advance your business.

6. *Find the best partner you can, but don't hold out for perfection.* The famed pianist Vladimir Horowitz once defended false notes in a performance in this way: "Perfection itself is imperfection." Overanalysis of the market will result only in a thorough understanding of which partner *was* the best one to have.

7. *Share a common vision with your partner.* Understand what makes your partner tick. Find partners who you can work with to help them achieve their goal, while they help you to achieve yours.

8. *Produce short-term wins.* Everyone likes to win. If you can show that a partnership produces results, even small ones, it will be easier to make a case for putting more resources into the deal.

9. *Create a long-term strategy even for short-term deals.* The bottom line is this: Don't make a deal for the sake of doing a deal. Every partnership you strike should help you achieve an end. The easier it is to communicate your strategy, the easier it should be to establish a framework that fits all deals, large and small.

10. *Consider proximity and distance as a part of the deal calculation.* Despite the Internet, the telephone, and high-speed transportation, location still matters. Often referred to as cluster economics, there are tangible and intangible benefits to being located in a strategic area where you can find complementary businesses.

Silicon Valley is known for high tech, Detroit for automobiles, and Wall Street for financial services. These are not geographic coincidences. If you find that you are making a lot of partnerships outside of your geographic area, then you should consider whether you are in the ideal location, or whether you have closely explored local alternatives.

Zooming Ahead

Tomorrow morning, as you pull out onto the road to the future, you will feel a familiar breeze in your face. It is the unrelenting wind of economic and technology-driven change, confronting not just you, but every manager trying to navigate his or her organization to success in the months and years ahead. My hope is that with the principles, case studies, and implementation tips detailed in this book, you will be well armed to lead the charge. Don't resist the wind; don't hope it fades away, because it will not. Experience it, embrace it, lean your shoulder into it. With the combination of the enduring, do-the-right-things-right principles of leadership, plus the new 6 factors for success, you have as clear a road map to the Next Economy as exists today. Enjoy the ride.

Sources

Interviews

I would like to thank each and every one of the business leaders who shared his or her time generously in contributing to this book. The principal interviews with each individual, the majority of which involved follow-up conversations, occurred as follows:

Peter Bell, StorageNetworks, August 14, 2000
Yobie Benjamin, Ernst and Young, June 23, 2000
John Chambers, Cisco Systems, August 10, 1998
Bill Coleman, BEA Systems, July 24, 2000; July 2, 2001
George Conrades, Akamai Technologies, May 26, 2000; July 3, 2001
Pat Garner, David and Tom Gardner, The Motley Fool, July 28, 2000
Mark Hoffman, Commerce One, October 23, 2000
Mark Hogan, General Motors/e-GM, September 25, 2000
Jeanne Jackson, Wal-Mart.com, October 6, 2000
Tim Koogle, Yahoo!, May 31, 2000
Geraldine Laybourne, Oxygen Media, August 7, 2000
Ted Lewis, Eastman Kodak, June 22, 2000
Gary Reiner, General Electric, April 19, 2000
Brian Swette, eBay, August 3, 2000
Jack Welch, General Electric, May 27, 1998

Meg Whitman, eBay, November 29, 2000
Ed Zander, Sun Microsystems, July 25, 2000

Periodicals and Journals

I would also like to extend my deep appreciation to the following periodicals and magazines, which every day, week, fortnight, or month produce information and insight that help keep readers at the cutting edge of the Next Economy. A number of the concepts and data (but none of the interviews or quotes) were drawn from many issues of the following:

Business Week
Business 2.0
Executive Excellence
Fast Company
Forbes
Fortune
Harvard Business Review
New York Times
Strategy & Business
The Wall Street Journal

Spencer Stuart Research Studies

The following pieces of intellectual capital formed much of the foundational research behind this book. They are all available on www.spencerstuart.com.

e-Quotient Survey
"Governance.com"
Internet Boards Index
"Talent.com," 1999
"The Great Migration"

Other Sources

U.S. Department of Commerce

MediaQuotient National Survey, 1999, and Anenberg Public Policy Center, 1999

Nielson Media Research, 1995

Books

Competing for the Future, Gary Hamel, C. K. Prahalad, Harvard Business School Press, 1994.

Faster: The Acceleration of Just About Everything, James Gleick, Pantheon Books, Random House, 1999.

The Friction-Free Economy, T. G. Lewis, Harper Business, 1997.

From Worst to First, Gordon Bethune, John Wiley, 1998.

Leadership Is an Art, Max Dupree, Dell Publishing, 1989.

The Leadership Moment, Michael Useem, Times Books, 1998.

Leadership Without Easy Answers, Ronald A. Heifetz, Belknap Press of Harvard University Press, 1994.

Lessons from the Top, Thomas J. Neff and James M. Citrin, Currency/Doubleday, 1999.

The Max Strategy: How a Businessman Got Stuck at an Airport and Learned to Make His Career Take Off, Dale Daunten, Quill, 1997.

MTV: The Making of a Revolution, Tom McGrath, Running Press, 1996.

Smart Alliances: A Practical Guide to Repeatable Success, John Harbison and Peter Pekar, Jr., Jossey-Bass, 1998.

A Social History of American Technology, Ruth Schwartz Cowan, Oxford University Press, 1996.

Speed Is Life: Street Smart Lessons from the Front Lines of Business, Bob Davis, Currency/Doubleday, 2001.

Zen and the Art of Motorcycle Maintenance, Robert M. Pirsig, William Morrow, 1974.

Acknowledgments

Creating a business book is more like producing a movie than sitting down and "writing" a book. It requires the orchestration of dozens of individuals sharing ideas, research, and reactions. In the case of *Zoom*, I have many leading and supporting "actors" to thank.

First, I would like to express my deep appreciation and affection to all of my colleagues at Spencer Stuart. Our firm is something special, where colleagues are good friends and work collegially together in teams serving our clients. For the past eight years, I have had the privilege of learning the art and science of executive search from the very best in our profession. The firm has supported me completely in striving to do great client work and also in my research on leadership both in the traditional and new economies. I would like to single out one of my mentors, Tom Neff, Spencer Stuart's U.S. chairman, who was my coauthor for *Lessons from the Top* and a true partner and friend in every sense of the word. In addition, I would like to thank another of my mentors, Carlton W. "Tony" Thompson, who has been a teacher, role model, and friend for many years and who has shared so much about the media and entertainment business from his vast reservoir of knowledge and relationships. I am also grateful to my dear friend and colleague Claudia Kelly, who in August 1993 suggested that I think about a career at Spencer Stuart. "You'd love our business," she said, "and be good at it too." She was so right—at least in the first part of her comment. And I want to express my deep gratitude to the Spencer Stuart top management team. CEO David Daniel; head of North America, Kevin Connelly; and head of Europe, Manuel Marquez, are all great friends and talented managers steering our firm successfully forward. Finally, there are two other colleagues whose friendship and support I deeply appreciate. First is Karen Steinegger, my administrative partner, who magically manages to get everything done on time with the highest quality imaginable. She has supported every aspect of my work at Spencer Stuart, including much of the thinking and all of the logistics involved in this book. The second is Jason Baumgarten, my "thought partner" for this book, whose bio is listed under "About the Author." Jason is one of the most intellectually gifted individuals I have ever met; but more important, he is genetically programmed to get things done. He conducted extensive research, analysis, and synthesis without which this book would not have been possible.

Many of the concepts in this book grew out of our research at Spencer Stuart (all available on www.Spencerstuart.com). The following is a list of the intellectual capital projects developed at our firm that laid the research foundation for this book:

- "Talent.com" was our breakthrough market study of 55 top companies at different stages of Internet deployment. Completed in 1999, Talent.com was the first study of its kind. The study taught us what goes into creating a winning Web-centric firm from an organizational and leadership perspective. Among the companies participating were Amazon.com, DoubleClick, eToys, Federal Express, Compaq, and Kodak.
- Our study "The Great Migration" tracked the movement of executive appointments from the traditional economy to the new economy since 1998. We measured the rate at which executives have come into the new economy, where they come from, and why. As a result, we have been able to learn why some managers succeed and others have had trouble adapting.
- Our annual *Internet Board* and *Compensation Surveys* have provided insight into best practices in corporate governance and established the market pricing for leadership in the Internet industry and the digital economy.

- Spencer Stuart's "Governance.com" study details how the role of boards of directors is changing in the digital economy and how they are helping companies and business leaders win.
- Our *e-Quotient Survey,* which provides a diagnostic tool to assess how satisfied and successful managers will be moving into the Internet industry.

I would like to thank Randall Rothenberg of consulting giant Booz Allen & Hamilton. Randy serves as both editor in chief of *Strategy & Business* and chief marketing officer for Booz Allen & Hamilton. Randy edited the original article "Digital Leadership" in the January 2000 issue of *Strategy & Business,* in which Tom Neff and I first introduced the concept that enduring principles of leadership, augmented by today's new principles of execution, are the key to success for companies going forward.

I also want to express my deepest appreciation to the clients of Spencer Stuart with whom I have the good fortune to work. Their support and partnership create a level of satisfaction seldom achieved in a professional setting. It is from this "leadership laboratory" of working with clients to build their top management teams that the greatest exposure to the best thinking about success occurs.

I would like to express my gratitude to all of the business leaders who agreed to participate in this book. They are listed individually in the Sources section. In addition, I want to thank the following individuals for helping me secure the following participants in this book: Jim Hebert of Sun Microsystems, who arranged for the Ed Zander (Sun Microsystems) and Peter Bell (StorageNetworks) interviews; Stewart Gross of Warburg, Pincus, who introduced me to Bill Coleman (BEA Systems); Dan Levitan of Maveron Equity Partners, who introduced me to Meg Whitman (eBay); John Flint of Polaris Venture Partners, who recommended me to George Conrades (Akamai Technologies); Jonathan White, managing director of Spencer Stuart's San Francisco office, who arranged for the Mark Hoffman (Commerce One) meeting; Rick Gostyla, co-managing director of Spencer Stuart's North American High Technology Practice, who helped arrange the John Chambers (Cisco Systems) interview; and Yobie Benjamin of Ernst and Young, who introduced me to Mark Hogan (General Motors/ e-GM). I would also like to express my appreciation to Kerry Christopher, communications manager at General Motors, who provided me with exceptional source material and editorial guidance to complement my one-on-one interviews. It is no small task to distill the transformational efforts of a $180 billion giant in several thousand words.

I would also like to acknowledge the fine work of Betsy Bowen, who transcribed the hundreds of hours of interviews into readable transcripts, and Byron Reimus, a consultant to Spencer Stuart, who continually feeds us provocative concepts and information and has worked with our firm's Internet Practice on our "Talent.com" and "Governance.com" projects. In addition, Bob Marston, Mike Milican, and Jim Horton of Robert Marston and Associates have provided invaluable advice and support on Spencer Stuart's public relations and corporate marketing front, as well as critical input into this book. An enormous amount of financial and shareholder return analysis helped distill the winning companies from the also-rans as well provide trends on the broader market and economy. I would like to thank Jay Genzer and Michael Rome from Lazard Asset Management for their generous contribution of data, analysis, and ideas. Jay and Michael also provided the financial analytical support that underpinned *Lessons from the Top*.

I would also like to thank the incredible support and literary contributions of my friend and literary agent Rafe Sagalyn. Rafe has the keen instincts of a top editor, as well as the rare ability to help put ideas together in a form that the reading public will (hopefully) find compelling. Another key partner in this enterprise is Paul B. Brown, whose special gift is to turn large volumes of transcripts and concepts into chapter drafts. A special thank-you must also go to Joshua Macht, a senior editor at Time Inc.'s *Business 2.0* magazine, who performed magic as the editor of this book. Josh's keen insights about technology and the Internet and corporate and individual behavior coupled with his extraordinary editorial skills made this book much better than it otherwise would have been.

To help bring the principles in *Zoom* to life in a memorable way visually, I turned to R. J. Matson, the award-winning illustrator for the *New York Observer*. R.J. worked closely with me to distill the essence from today's best business practices and communicate them in simple but highly original ways. Taking all of the efforts of this extended team to the next level is the Currency/Doubleday team led by executive editor Roger Scholl. Roger's exacting standards and commitment to quality are enormously appreciated. Working with Roger results in a keen feeling of satisfaction.

Finally, my deepest thanks and affection go to my best friend and wife, Gail Citrin, and our three children, Teddy (11), Oliver (9), and Lily (6), who are the true loves of my life. They had the patience and love to support this effort, which had to be expended over and above a normally heavy professional workload. And in my search for just the right title for the book, the kids were big supporters of *Zoom*.

Index

Page numbers of illustrations, graphs, and tables appear in italics.

James M. Citrin is managing director of Spencer Stuart's Global Technology, Communications, and Media Practice. In 1999, he founded the firm's Global Internet Practice, and in 1996 founded the firm's Media and Communications Practice. Citrin is also chairman of Spencer Stuart Talent Network, the Internet-powered recruiting service focusing on connecting emerging executive leadership with the world's best companies. Over his eight years at Spencer Stuart, Citrin has completed over 210 executive search assignments. He specializes in CEO searches for a wide range of clients in high technology, entertainment, publishing, the Internet, telecommunications, consumer products, and hospitality.

Major CEO placements include Yahoo! Inc., Reader's Digest Association, Primedia, Gruner & Jahr USA Publishing, L. L. Bean, Bertelsmann's BOL.com, ClubMom, Frictionless Commerce, Holiday Inn Worldwide, and The John and Mary R. Markle Foundation. Major president and COO placements include Eastman Kodak Company, Akamai Technologies, Barnesandnoble.com, Discovery Communications, and Penguin Publishing.

Outside of his executive search practice, Citrin is a leading commentator and expert on leadership, governance, and human capital issues. He is coauthor of *Lessons from the Top: The Search for America's Best Business Leaders* (Doubleday 1999), which has been published in six languages. Citrin is also a columnist for Time Inc.'s *Business 2.0* magazine, where he contributes a bi-weekly column, "Talent Monger," on the Web site www.business2.com as well as in the magazine. Citrin has published articles on leadership, corporate governance, and recruiting CEOs to early-stage companies in the *New York Times, Strategy & Business, Directors & Boards,* and many other publications. He has been widely interviewed on these topics on NBC, CNBC, CNN, National Public Radio, USA Radio Network, and the Voice of America, and in *Business Week* and *Fortune* magazines among others.

Prior to joining Spencer Stuart, Citrin was director of corporate planning at Reader's Digest Association, with responsibility for long-range planning, acquisitions, and strategic alliances. Before that, he was a senior engagement manager with McKinsey & Company, both in the United States and France. Earlier, Citrin was an associate with Goldman, Sachs & Co., and before attending graduate business school, a financial analyst with Morgan, Stanley & Co.

A graduate of Vassar College, Phi Beta Kappa, with a B.A. in economics, Citrin obtained an M.B.A. from the Harvard Business School, where he graduated with distinction. Citrin is a director of the Nasdaq company Dice Inc. and serves as a trustee of Vassar College. He is also a member of the Board of the Harvard Business School Club of New York and is a senior advisor with the Seattle-based Maveron Equity Partners.

Citrin lives in New Canaan, Connecticut, with his wife, Gail, and their three children, Teddy, Oliver, and Lily.

Jason Baumgarten is vice president of strategy and new product development for Spencer Stuart Talent Network, where he oversees strategy and ongoing research and development efforts. Prior to this role, Jason was a key member of Spencer Stuart's Global Internet Practice. His work regarding compensation and talent trends has been cited frequently in *The Wall Street Journal,* and he has been quoted in various publications including *The Industry Standard, dotCEO, Red Herring, Chief Executive, CFO Magazine, InfoWorld,* and *Crain's New York Business.* Before joining Spencer Stuart, Jason held various positions at a major advertising firm, a retail brokerage firm, and an independent film production company. He also served as the station manager of a not-for-profit radio station. Jason, a graduate of Vassar College, with a B.A. in economics, served as the president of the student government. He lives in Greenwich, Connecticut.

Paul B. Brown is the author of several business bestsellers, including *Customers for Life* (written with Carl Sewell; Doubleday/Currency), which has been translated into fifteen languages and has sold more than 800,000 copies worldwide. He collaborated with James M. Citrin and coauthor Thomas J. Neff on *Lessons from the Top*. Brown is a former writer and editor for *Business Week, Forbes, Financial World,* and *Inc.* He lives with his wife, son, and daughter on Cape Cod Bay and in New Jersey.